RMCUST/06

Contagious
Customer
Care

First published in Great Britain in 2001 by
Go MAD Books
Pocket Gate Farm
Off Breakback Road
Woodhouse Eaves
Leicestershire
LE12 8RS

British Library Cataloguing in Publication Data.
A catalogue record for this book is available from the
British Library.

ISBN 0-9537284-5-5

Printed and bound in Great Britain by
Cox & Wyman, Reading

ACKNOWLEDGEMENTS

If we were to individually thank all the people who have contributed to this book you would spend the next fifteen minutes reading a list of names. We'll start as we mean to go on and keep the acknowledgements short, sweet and easy to read! However there are a number of people we simply must mention...

We would like to thank Professor David Wilson at Warwick University for his help, advice and guidance in the early stages of this project, and are particularly grateful for his support and encouragement.

Very, very special thanks go to all those people we have interviewed in the process of researching and writing this book. You were all great and make our jobs that extra bit special. We feel privileged to have met so many fascinating and inspiring individuals.

Many thanks go to all the organisations that contributed to this research. In particular we would like to express our appreciation to the following:

Guilbert UK Ltd
Homebase
Royal and SunAlliance
RS Components

You made us feel very welcome, provided us with comfortable space to carry out our interviews and copious amounts of coffee - excellent customer service!

To the rest of the Go MAD team, our families and friends –
you all know who you are – what would we do without you?
Your patience knows no bounds, your support is absolute.

The thanks go on and on…but we won't!

**"To laugh often and much; to win the respect of
intelligent people and the affection of children; to
earn the appreciation of honest critics and endure the
betrayal of false friends; to appreciate beauty; to find
the best in others; to leave the world a bit better,
whether by a healthy child, a garden patch or a
redeemed social condition; to know even one life has
breathed easier because you have lived.
This is to have succeeded."
Ralph Waldo Emerson**

Contents

BUILD EFFECTIVE RELATIONSHIPS WITH YOUR CUSTOMERS

POSITIVE ATTITUDES

BE SOLUTION FOCUSED – THINK OF ALL YOUR POSSIBILITIES

BE PART OF A WINNING TEAM

KEEPING PROMISES

SERVICE RECOVERY

THE UNPREDICTABLE X FACTOR IN CUSTOMER CARE

SOME FINAL THOUGHTS

YOU'VE READ THE BOOK – SO WHAT NEXT?

"The mediocre teacher tells. The good teacher explains. The superior teacher demonstrates. The great teacher inspires."
William Arthur Ward

INTRODUCTION

1. Hello and welcome to Contagious Customer Care

**"Contagious - likely to effect others
(contagious enthusiasm)."
Readers Digest Oxford Complete Wordfinder**

This book has been written for people who want to make a difference in customer care. We have purposefully made it easy to read and digest. We wanted to be able to talk to you, and not at you, about great customer care. With this in mind we created a book that we could share with you as friends and fellow service providers. It is different to other books you might have read. It is written in a casual style - very much as if we were writing to friends. We want you to enjoy the novelty of a book written both about you, and for you. It's not supposed to provide the answers to every question you ever had about customer service. It's designed to give you food for thought and help you to make a difference. Read on and be inspired!

**"What lies behind us and what lies before us are tiny
matters compared to what lies within us."
Oliver Wendell Holmes**

Three people were involved in the researching, writing and production of this book. We combined our skills and experience to bring you inspirational stories about fantastic customer care and the people who delivered it. We will also share with you examples, hints, tips and strategies used in customer service by the people we have met over the years.

2. Who exactly are we?

We are a team of consultants from Go MAD Ltd, a training and organisational development company that specialises in helping people to understand and develop their ability to make a difference. We achieve this by: undertaking research projects; providing training and coaching solutions; and providing help, guidance and support to organisations through a range of text, audio and e-learning development materials.

Ian has a background in both education and the commercial world. He joined Go MAD Ltd and combined his experience in these two distinct fields, developing his expertise in cultural and organisational change. He works with organisations to help them understand the roles that behaviours have to play, both internally and externally, when developing a customer-focused environment. Ian's role takes him into both the private and public sector. He also continues to work within education helping young people to develop the personal skills they need in order to make a difference.

Alison joined Go MAD Ltd after spending eleven years in the insurance industry. She spent seven years involved in a variety of customer care roles. The latter four years saw Alison developing a passion for training and development. This change in career direction led to her taking on the role of Training and Development Manager for a large international organisation. Her expertise includes experience from within a customer-facing environment, as well as her training and development knowledge. Alison specialises in achieving sustained performance improvement, change management, leadership development and one to one coaching.

Nicky joined Ian, Alison and the rest of the Go MAD team to bring expertise in the area of research and psychology. She holds a BSc degree in Social Psychology, and has a particular interest in the psychology of work. Nicky is also well read in the area of customer service, and has experienced a variety of customer facing roles, including that of a Registered General Nurse! She brings with her a wealth of personal customer care experiences, research, and analytical skills.

3. What is your reason why?

Firstly, we've made one huge assumption; if you're reading this book you must have more than a passing interest in customer care! You are already that little bit different – you cared enough to pick up a book designed to help you excel.

Whoever you are, and whatever your job, somewhere along the line you deal with customers. You may have direct face-to-face contact with external customers, or your customers may be your colleagues. Whatever your focus, the importance of customer satisfaction is inescapable.

Maybe you're eager to learn new ways to make a difference to your customers; maybe you'd like to consolidate what you already know. Perhaps you are looking for some inspiration or are simply compelled to read every book on customer service you can lay your hands on! Whatever your reason, you will gain value from this book – it's designed to make you smile, think and feel. Most of all it's designed to develop your passion for customer care.

"Get a life...Get a reason why."
Andy Gilbert

---

4. Make a difference

You will find throughout this book that we use the term *'make a difference'* with regularity. Making a difference is what we are all about. Since 1997 we have specialised in researching the process of natural success and how individuals can improve their ability to make a difference in their lives. From this ongoing research, a set of seven key principles have been identified which link together to form a simple, yet sophisticated, success framework with a multi-purpose application. Andy Gilbert, Group Managing Director of Go MAD Ltd, coined the phrase Go MAD® (Go Make A Difference) to describe this as the natural process of success.

Whilst the customer care research for this book was conducted separately from the ongoing research carried out by the team at Go MAD Ltd, we have found that the Go MAD® process was naturally applied by the people we interviewed. Without exception the seven key principles of Go MAD® formed the basis for the consistent delivery of excellent customer care.

As this book isn't designed to tell you how to deliver excellent customer care, we won't be presenting the Go MAD® model in it's entirety. If you are interested in this process of success, Go MAD® is explained in depth in Andy's book 'Go MAD - The Art of Making A Difference'.

5.   What you *will* encounter in this book

In the early stages of this project, one of the first questions we asked ourselves was, "How can we inspire people and develop their passion for customer care?" It made sense for us to collect stories. Stories which would highlight and inspire excellence in customer care. The next question was "How do we get the right stories?"

We decided to do this in several ways. We approached organisations and asked them to nominate employees who they felt consistently excelled in customer care. Every day, in some way, the individuals nominated make a difference to the customers they came into contact with. They are not necessarily company 'high-fliers', but are people who are genuinely passionate about customer care.

We interviewed the nominees and asked them to tell us about times when they felt they had really exceeded their customer's expectations. By carrying out these in-depth interviews we were able to gather evidence on strategies used in excellent customer service. We found out how people had overcome obstacles while meeting their customer's needs; ways in which customer's expectations had been exceeded; and how, in many different ways, these people had made a difference to their customers.

We took the opportunity to audio record and analyse the content of the interviews with these role models. Our next task was to identify the stories we felt best reflected the underlying ethos surrounding fantastic customer care.

We also asked customers to tell us their stories to supplement the contributions made by those who provided the care. Our own experiences complete the picture to provide you with further insight and ideas. So, this book is full of real examples of inspirational customer care. Stories told by real people about real events.

"Live and learn and pass it on."

---

6. More about the book

We also wanted this book to be a practical 'doing' book. Alongside the stories are learning points, hints and tips. There are also development exercises for you to do – most of which are designed to stimulate your thoughts and focus you on a tangible difference to make. You obviously don't have to complete these. Unless of course you're *really* serious about improving your customer care. The very act of writing will ensure that you think more deeply about the points we raise.

As with all Go MAD® books, we actively encourage you to pick up a pen, write on the pages, jot down your thoughts and take part in the exercises. Make the most of what we offer you. We recognise that some people prefer not to write in a book. Perhaps you might be worried that someone else may pick up your book and read your notes. Maybe you have a deep-seated memory of being scolded as a child for writing in your books! If this is the case use a separate piece of paper. Alternatively you can choose to shake your inhibitions – write in the book, underline words, make notes and highlight sections which are particularly applicable to you.

7. Our favourite quotes

Interspersed throughout the book, gathered from a variety of sources, are some of our favourite inspirational quotes relating to the points covered in each section. Some you may agree with; some you may not. The intention is that they will prompt your thoughts. Why not start your own collection of inspirational quotes?

One of our particular favourites about customer care is:

"Worry about being better; bigger will take care of itself. Think one customer at a time and take care of each one the best way you can."
Gary Comer

---

8. More things for you to do

At the end of each section we will suggest three actions you can take to help you make a difference in customer service. These actions will relate to the points we have made in the preceding section. They are intended to give you practical ways to transfer your learning from the book to your work situation. You will possibly already be doing some of them – that's great, keep it up! Other actions may not appeal to you and with some you'll be itching to put them into place. Whatever your reaction, the three actions offer you the posibility of making a tangible difference.

**"Don't put off until tomorrow
what you can do today."**

---

9. Ways to approach using this book

As with most things in life, there is more than just one way
to use this book. Although we encourage you to do every
development exercise and put into place every action point,
we realise that not every aspect of the book may be
appropriate for you. For a start you may believe that you
already deliver excellent customer care!

Perhaps you would like to share your learning with a friend,
a colleague or members of your team. Maybe you can think
of someone who is in dire need of some direction in the
delivery of excellent customer care. Ultimately it is your
choice – it is your responsibility!

**"Choice, not chance,
determines the difference you make."**
Andy Gilbert

The following points are offered to help you get the most
from this book. You may want to:

● Read it all through first, highlighting the learning points
that are most applicable to you. You can then refer to
them as and when the fancy takes you!

● Read it all through, highlighting the development
activities you wish to complete. Then go back to the

beginning and do the activities in one go – or over a period of time.

● Read through the whole book completing all the development activities.

● Refer to the index of stories (pages 175 – 178). You can simply browse the list of 29 stories and see which ones grab your attention. Go straight to those that interest you and enjoy their inspirational message.

● Just dip in and out of the book. That's the beauty of having such short chapters!

Whichever method you use is fine. Just make sure it's the right one for you.

**"You can steer yourself in any direction you choose.
You're on your own. And you know what you know.
You are the guy who'll decide where to go."
Dr. Seuss**

---

10. Customer service or customer care?

You will notice throughout this book that we refer to both customer service and customer care. You may believe that there is a difference between these two concepts or you may feel that they are one and the same. Although we readily accept this, we have decided to use both terms! We feel that in many cases their use is a matter of personal choice. So as you read please feel free to replace one with the other, as you prefer.

"Great changes may not happen right away,
but with effort even the difficult
become easy."
Bill Blackman

CUSTOMER CARE –
IS THERE A DEFINITION?

11. What is excellent customer care?

A simple enough question – what is excellent customer care? You may have already asked yourself this question. One thing we are sure of – customer care is not a new concept. It's applicable in any organisation and to all employees.

Before you read any further, please take the time to complete the following exercise.

PICK UP YOUR PEN

Write down in a few words your definition of delivering excellent customer care.

Excellent customer care is:

You may have found this exercise easy to complete. Perhaps you have already got a definite idea of what constitutes excellence in customer care. You might have based your response around a company service statement or your own beliefs. Many people express their definitions along the lines of *"satisfying or exceeding my customers needs"*. Obviously there is not one definitive answer to the question of what is customer service. However, it is important to have a personal view and be able to recognise what it means for your organisation.

Your organisation may have the best products, the best pricing, the best choice, and the best marketing, but without great customer care it will risk losing everything. Organisations are becoming more aware of the need to compete both in terms of the products they offer and the service they deliver.

RS Components has a long history of excellence in customer care; the very foundations of the business were based on reliability, efficiency and genuine care. We invited Diane Knight, Head of UK Human Resources for RS, to contribute a brief history of what customer care means to her organisation.

> Principles of exceptional customer service date back to the company's origins in 1937, when founders Paul Sebestyen and Herbert Waring identified the need for a fast supply of low cost radio parts. They were determined to provide a customer service no one else could match. Radio retailers had been finding it hard to source spares for service and repair of the new Marconi invention. Sebestyen and Waring, who had been looking for a new business opportunity, stepped in to meet the demand.

Retailers were offered same-day despatch of spares, helping to breathe new life into the radios of the nation. Twenty-four hour dispatch was continued through the toughest days of the Second World War, as home radio sets were relied upon to broadcast news from the battlefront. After the war the reputation of Radiospares (forerunner of RS Components) grew stronger still as it built on a solid foundation of excellent customer service and a proud background of reliability, loyalty and trust.

The company's customer service was so highly regarded that in the 1950's industries outside the radio world requested supplies, eventually leading to growth and expansion, both nationally and internationally. The RS brand is now recognised and respected around the world by both customers and suppliers.

The earliest customer service principles of RS still hold true in today's global organisation. A determination to succeed is based on a firm resolve never to be beaten on service. As Head of Human Resources, I know how much we rely on the excellence and enthusiasm of our people to maintain our unique success in serving our customers so well. This is why our employees are so important to our business, and they know that unbeatable service is paramount to a successful future. They also learn to treat colleagues from other departments as customers in their own right in a spirit of cross-company unity and cooperation, designed to maximise achievement.

Employees work diligently to meet every customer demand, and customer convenience is everything. Innovative products and solutions delivered by RS Components will continue to be matched only by further innovations in supreme customer care.

**"Perfection is our goal,
excellence will be tolerated."
Jay Goltz**

It didn't matter who we asked in our research, all agreed that customer service is paramount to business success. It may be regarded as an obvious necessity – but how many organisations actually live by their beliefs? Unlike RS Components, many organisations claim to deliver first class customer service, yet they often fall short of their promises and fail to meet their customer's expectations.

**"All I got in this world is my balls and my word and I
don't break either of 'em for nobody!"
Al Pacino, 'Scarface'**

---

12.   What does customer care mean to you?

No matter how grand organisational policies and guidelines are, without the right people to deliver them the policies are worthless. Let's focus on you, the person who makes it happen.

You're a customer – how many times have you received the service you expect? How much time have you spent looking for a sales assistant to help you – only to find a gaggle of them locked in deep conversation? Have you ever taken time off work to wait at home for that special delivery or trades person to repair something? And as the day draws to a close you finally admit to yourself they are not coming! How long have you spent waiting in a bank or supermarket queue? Have you ever been scowled at by a checkout operator and made to feel a nuisance as you packed away your groceries?

Do any of these scenarios sound familiar? They have happened to us many times.

PICK UP YOUR PEN

Now consider excellent customer care from the point of view of a customer. How do you expect to be treated? You have already defined what excellent customer care is (page 21) – now define what it means to you when you are on the receiving end of service.

> When I am a customer, excellent customer care means:

There may, or may not, be a difference between your descriptions. Consider the difference between what organisations, and customers, believe to be excellent customer service. Let us assure you, some companies are definitely barking up the wrong tree! Consider this – excellent customer care is finding out what each individual customer's definition of excellent customer care is and then having the flexibility to tailor the care you deliver to their specific needs.

"Never take anything for granted."
Benjamin Disraeli

ASK YOURSELF

- To what extent are my definitions of excellent customer care based on organisational policy or how I really feel?

- What could I do to treat each of my customers uniquely?

- What assumptions do I make about how my customers would like to be treated? Do I actually take the time to find out?

These questions may have prompted you to rethink your definitions of excellent customer care. Please feel free to go back and alter your definition if you have changed your perceptions.

13. Who are your customers?

Who exactly are your customers? What if everybody has the potential of being your customer? The concept certainly shouldn't be kept for those people in direct customer facing roles, e.g. the sales person, checkout operator or receptionist.

Customer service is applicable to everyone. It refers to both the service given to external customers and the service delivered between internal departments within your organisation. Your colleagues, your boss, your managers and ultimately the directors of your organisation are all responsible for delivering internal customer service. For some their role may be entirely focused on internal service delivery; for others the majority of their contact may be with the public or corporate customers. A useful way for you to consider who your customers are is summed up in the quote below.

"Your customer is the person you are trying to help."
Source Unknown

"The heights by great men reached and kept
were not obtained by sudden flight.
But they, while their companions slept,
were toiling upwards in the night."
Thomas S. Manson

COMMUNICATE WITH YOUR CUSTOMER

Bob Fitzsimmons's story

Unique needs

In the latter months of the year 2000 several areas of the UK faced severe flooding. Whole communities were left shattered in the wake of the receding floodwaters.

Bob Fitzsimmons, Claims Advisor Service Manager at Royal and SunAlliance described the devastation that met him and his team as they assembled at Lewes, one of the most badly hit areas in the UK. *"People were out on the streets trying to salvage what they could from their houses. In some cases diesel and raw sewage were flooding through their property. It is hard to describe the complete desolation that was felt by this community. In the space of a few hours, homes that had taken a life time to build were destroyed and precious belongings were ruined."*

If you had been dealt this terrible blow what would have helped you? Bob believes strongly that he should seek individual solutions for each customer. *"It wasn't about insurance policies at this stage, it's about helping people through one of the most traumatic events of their lives. It never ceases to amaze me that we are in the position to make a difference in peoples lives when they are at such a low ebb."*

Power and telephone lines were down in Lewes when Bob first arrived. The first thing he did was to set up a huge mobile emergency centre in heart of Lewes. He arranged for the press team of Royal & SunAlliance to involve the local radio and TV stations. Bob gave interviews to the media and ensured the community knew that Royal & SunAlliance were there to help. Building contractors, claims advisors, and disaster restoration companies worked together as one big team. Bob described how the service they were offering went beyond their customers to the wider community. They readily offered advice and support to people insured by their competitors. For their own customers they were able to do so much more.

Take, for example, the elderly couple whose home had suffered from the worst of the flooding. They were not coping at all well with the chaos surrounding them. Instead of arranging for them to stay in a local hotel, Bob suggested that they might like to holiday abroad for a month at Royal & SunAlliance's expense. Yes we were surprised at this too, but as Bob pointed out, the weather was cold and typically British; every time the couple watched the news reports they were reliving their experiences. They couldn't escape the awful reality of their situation and were just not coping.

After assessing their individual situation, Bob felt that they would benefit from taking a break in the sun, rather than spending a miserable few weeks watching and waiting for their home to be restored. The cost to Royal & SunAlliance would be the same and Bob had come up with an individual solution for these particular customers.

Bob explained that in this particular case his customers gratefully handed over full control to him. Royal &

SunAlliance arranged access for builders, cleansing contractors and restoration workers to enter their home and repair the damage. In other cases his customers desperately wanted to remain involved – if necessary Bob telephoned them two or three times a day to let them know how things were progressing, *"I will do whatever it takes to reassure my customers. If this means phoning them every hour on the hour then this is what I will do."*

14. You have to communicate to appreciate

This brief example illustrates how important it is for you to communicate with your customers. Without adequate communication there is little chance of you appreciating their unique needs.

Bob and his team didn't assume that each of the Lewes flood victims would require the same assistance. Instead they took the time to communicate with them all on an individual basis. The team were able to bring help, comfort and understanding at a time when they needed it most.

"It's good to talk!"
British Telecom

---

15. Make yourself available to your customers

In order to establish how best you can understand your customer's unique needs you must first consider the context of your interactions with them. Consider each situation in which you have contact with your customers and then consider your options.

Take, for example, Bob's case. His contact involved walking the streets of the devastated Lewes looking for people who needed his help. He answered phone calls, knocked on his customers doors, distributed leaflets, made himself available at the mobile emergency centre and gave interviews to both radio and television stations, all in the effort to ensure his customers knew his team were there for them.

Bob explored every avenue he had in order to make contact with his customers. He exercised the first golden rule of communication – he made himself available!

How available are you to your customers? The list below is designed to help you consider just how many times you make contact with your customers.

A customer may:

- telephone you
- approach you while you're working
- be waiting for you to arrive
- approach the help desk you are working at
- be waiting for you to approach them
- sit next to you in the staff canteen
- write or e-mail you
- ask for directions
- put their goods through your checkout
- park their car next to yours in the staff car park
- be seated at the table you wait on

There will be many other forms of contact that will be unique to each situation. Each one of these situations demands different levels of communication. However, all of them constitute opportunities for you to really understand your customer's uniqueness.

PICK UP YOUR PEN

Be creative; think of at least five more situations where you have contact with your customers.

I have contact with my customers:

16. Clear communication

Now you have considered the circumstances in which you have contact with your customers (remembering that they could be internal or external), it's time to consider how you communicate with them.

At its most basic, communication involves the sender and a recipient. Imagine the sender is your customer and the recipient is you! Your customers will send you many different messages. For example, you may be approached on a shop floor and asked if you have a particular item in stock. This message is clear and you are able to answer a specific question.

What would have happened if a customer approached you, obviously looking harassed, and searching for a 'thingamabob' to do the painting with? Obviously this is not such an easy message to understand. If the message from your customer is indistinct, the wrong actions may be taken. However, it's not the customer's job to make sure their message is clear, it's your job to interpret what your customer really needs.

**"Communicate – impart, convey;
reveal – give or exchange information."
Collins Gem English Dictionary**

The interpretation of your customer's needs can range from being straightforward to notoriously difficult. If a customer asks you a specific question, more often than not it's obvious what their needs are. However, sometimes you may be in situations similar to Bob's. His customers were going through a very traumatic time in their lives. Some of their needs were obvious, for example, they all needed cleansing services to rid their homes of the floodwater. Other needs were far subtler. Bob spoke at length to the elderly couple – they didn't ask to be flown abroad! They simply described their anxiety, hopelessness and despair to Bob. They told him how they kept reliving the nightmare of the flood every time they saw an article in a paper or news report on TV. The devastation was all around them. Bob told us how in situations similar to this he thinks about how he would want one of his relatives treated. As well as practical help, they needed physical and emotional assistance too. Bob's solution was to offer them the holiday. This wasn't standard procedure; it was a unique solution, for a unique customer, in unique circumstances.

17. Non-verbal communication

Another key skill relating to communication is recognising and acting on the non-verbal behaviours of your customers. As individuals, we use our whole bodies when we communicate and non-verbal communication serves a number of purposes. It helps us to communicate how we feel and what we want, for example, facial displays of basic emotions, such as happiness, sadness, disgust, anger, surprise and fear are powerful communicators.

Non-verbal communication (or clues) can help you understand your customer's needs. For example, a customer may look confused; they may have a furrowed brow; they might be referring to some scribbled notes; and they might even be scratching their heads! One thing that is obvious in this scenario is that they need your help.

In the same way you interpret your customers non-verbal behaviour, they will interpret yours. For example, are you continually aware of customers entering your sphere of influence? Do you smile when they approach you? Such a small gesture can make such a huge difference.

**"A smile is the curve that sets everything straight."
Phyllis Diller**

---

18. Communicating by telephone with your customers

We are sure by now that you might be thinking that all this makes sense – but what about when you are dealing with customers over the phone?

We recognise that if a majority of your dealings with customers are over the phone, or via some other form of technology, you don't have all the benefits of non-verbal clues. But think about it for a moment – you do have some clues to work with. Listen closely to your customer's voice. Is their tone confident? Do they stumble over their words? Do they sound anxious or bright and cheerful? Use your ears and tune into the emotional content and tone of your customer's voice.

Other clues to watch out for include:

● A hurried tone. Your customer is in a rush – be quick and efficient, they haven't the time for chit chat.

● A pleading tone. Your customer is desperate for your help.

● An inquiring tone. Your customer has questions for you.

These clues, in addition to the message that your customer is communicating, will give you a greater understanding of their specific needs.

PICK UP YOUR PEN

Think about times when you have communicated with your customers, both in face-to-face situations and via the telephone. Even written communication can reveal helpful clues, for example, letters written in a sarcastic, angry, cheerful or confused tone will give you clues about the mood of the sender.

Use the space below to make a note of the clues you have previously encountered in your contact with customers. Also make a note of the clues you could look out for.

Clues I have previously encountered:

Clues I could look out for:

19.   Making a difference using the telephone

Deborah's story, featured below, highlights the differences you can make to your customers using the telephone as a method of communication. Deborah's customer gave her a clear description of the breakdown in their production line which, when combined with the desperate tone of her customer's voice, prompted Deborah into unusual action. She appreciated her customer's unique circumstances, and took unique steps to satisfy their needs.

Deborah Stewart's Story

Understanding your customers needs

Would you have the confidence to challenge company policy? Deborah Stewart did after she received a phone call from a customer situated in the docklands of Belfast, Northern Ireland. The customer's production line had experienced a significant breakdown and for every hour the system stood still, considerable revenue was being lost. Although the RS Components trade counter where Deborah worked offered a couriered delivery service, Deborah and the customer involved were both aware that this facility wasn't available overseas. In normal circumstances parts would take approximately forty-eight hours to get to Belfast.

Would you consider these circumstances acceptable? Deborah didn't, and she posed herself a question, was it possible for her to get the part to the customer within twenty-four hours? Yes of course it was. The next question she asked herself was how she was going to do it!

Deborah made a quick decision. She arranged for a courier to take the parts to Birmingham airport and booked them onto a flight to Belfast City airport, where the delighted and relieved customer collected them. Deborah said, *"It was so satisfying, solving a problem, the customer was desperate for the part, I simply thought is this possible? I could do it, so I did it."* Deborah is convinced that strong working relationships are formed in this way, fostering trust, confidence and loyalty from customers.

20. Don't assume you understand

In all of the communications you have with your customers it is important that you really understand what their needs are. Don't assume you understand; don't assume that they will be able to express their needs adequately, and always check your information carefully. If you have a doubt in your mind ask your customer, paraphrase their questions and confirm what they require.

"The secret of success is the ability to put yourself in another person's shoes, and to consider things from his or her point of view as well as your own."
Henry Ford

THREE ACTIONS FOR YOU TO CONSIDER

1. Smile when you are on the telephone.

2. Ask your customers what their preferred method of

communication is, for example, the telephone, fax, email or letter, and use that method wherever possible.

3. Confirm actions in writing with your customer to enhance your communication.

SECTION SUMMARY

- Communicate with your customers and appreciate their unique circumstances.

- Consider the situations in which you have contact with your customers and then consider the options you have to communicate with them.

- Interpret your customers' needs accurately, provide unique solutions, for unique customers, in unique circumstances.

- Make the most of non-verbal clues when you communicate with your customers.

- Use your ears and tune into the emotional content and tone of your customers' voice.

- Don't assume you understand the needs of your customers – ask! Paraphrase their questions and confirm what they require.

BUILD EFFECTIVE RELATIONSHIPS WITH YOUR CUSTOMERS

21. Establish a rapport with your customers

You have the opportunity to build an effective rapport with every customer you interact with. Every response you give to a customer does make a difference – you will leave them all with an impression. Whether the impression is positive or negative is up to you.

The contact you have with your customers can vary from a single telephone conversation to continuous contact over a number of years. Obviously you have more of an opportunity to build strong relationships with your customers over a period of time. However, don't neglect your responses to a single telephone conversation. They can make the difference between a customer returning or going elsewhere with their custom.

"You can have the best product and the best place on the high street – but if the people aren't right you won't be successful."
Paul Bridle

---

22. Make a connection with your customers

Kieran Dowling, whose story is featured below, understands the importance of making a connection with each of his individual customers. He goes to great lengths to cultivate a strong working relationship with them all.

Kieran's story

Building strong relationships

Who are our customers?….. A question asked frequently by organisations. Kieran Dowling, Transport Manager at Guilbert UK Ltd, believes that his customers are more than just a corporate identity. He argues that every employee of Guilbert's clients are his personal customers too.

Think about that for a moment. If you trade with a self-employed retailer, that's one customer. If you trade with the likes of British Airways, that's over 30,000 potential customers and if you trade with a retail giant such as Tesco, that's over 120,000 potential customers. Rather than finding this concept intimidating, Kieran believes this is a great opportunity in which to make a positive impact on each individual he, and his department, encounters.

Kieran has developed several unique customer procedures for his transport division. For example, after a customer introduction through the Guilbert account managers, Kieran arranges to meet the individuals, within the customer's business, with whom his drivers will be coming into day-to-day contact with. He feels that it is important to meet those people who will have direct contact with the transport division – not the sales teams or buyers – the individuals his drivers will be delivering to. In most cases these are the Warehouse Managers and their staff.

He then arranges to visit his customers with the regular driver of that particular geographical route. On his visit he builds a personal relationship with those people who will actually deal with his drivers. He checks preferences for delivery times, vehicle loadings and delivery points, and enquires if there is anything his drivers could do that would make life easier for the customer. He introduces the driver to the customer's team and ensures that all the customer's needs are communicated to that driver. Finally, in the unlikely event of a problem occurring, he makes certain that the customer has his direct line telephone number.

Kieran is well aware that his customers are the individuals who work for the company he trades with. Keeping each one of them happy requires an investment of his time, in getting to know them and establishing their needs, in order to excel in delivering the service the customer wants.

23. Putting in the groundwork

There are certain steps you need to take in order to establish a relationship with your customers.

Step one: Be friendly to your customers

Treat your customers as friends; offer them the same courtesy and understanding you offer to those you socialise with. Be approachable - exude warmth and friendliness. Maintain eye contact with your customers and keep a relaxed open stance. Remember, just because your customer can't see you, it doesn't mean that they can't tell if you smile at them down the phone - customers interpret non-verbal clues too!

Step two: Invest time in your customers

Make a good impression and your customers will return. You may only spend a few minutes with them – but you can make those minutes count. Put yourself in your customer shoes for a moment! If you approach an assistant in a DIY store and ask for the location of the barbeques – what would you be most impressed by? The assistant who, with an obligatory smile, points you in the right direction or the assistant who genuinely smiles at you and takes the time to accompany you to the appropriate section, chatting about how much fun barbeques can be.

A vast majority of us will prefer the latter approach. The sales assistant in this scenario went out of their way to make you feel valued. They dedicated a small amount of their time and did what they could to assist you in the store. Even the briefest encounter can leave your customer with a positive impression.

Step three: Listen and empathise with your customers

Listening is an active process. You need to channel your concentration onto the customer you are dealing with. Block out signals that interfere with this process. It could be a phone ringing next to you; it could be conversations happening between colleagues – whatever the interruption to your listening block it out.

Don't interrupt your customer – let them have their say. Don't leap to conclusions too soon. When your customer has finished speaking, ask them questions to clarify their needs. Do empathise with your customers and understand their particular circumstances.

**"When people talk, listen completely.
Most people never listen."
Ernest Hemingway**

---

24. Put theory into practice

Kieran employs all three of the steps we have described. He takes time to visit his customers. He maintains a friendly and courteous manner. He listens and empathises with his customers. He appreciates that each individual may have different needs. He doesn't assume that he knows best – he asks his customers questions to confirm their needs. Finally he leaves them with his direct line telephone number in case they need further assistance.

**"He who gives great service gets great returns."
Elbert Hubbard**

PICK UP YOUR PEN

Spend a few minutes reflecting on the things you presently do to form relationships with your customers. Ask yourself the following questions:

- How do I greet a customer when they approach me?
- How do I identify my customers needs?
- How do I respond to my customers needs?
- How well do I listen to my customer?
- What impression do I give to my customers?

Now list six things you could do to strengthen your relationships with your customers.

Six steps I could take to strengthen my relationship with customers include:

"The final measure of quality customer service is simply how the customer perceives it."

---

25. Maintain relationships with your customers

Consider yourself an individual spoke in a large wheel; you really can help to maintain relationships with all of your internal and external customers. You can make the difference. You have the power to make, or break, a customer relationship.

In some circumstances, you may not personally meet a customer again following your initial contact. However, it's important not to underestimate the significance of your exchange. You may have been part of the first experience that an individual had with your organisation. In this circumstance the impression you left with them will become the foundation for all further dealings they have with your organisation. You can lay the foundation stone of a strong lasting relationship. If, however, you left a particularly bad impression the chances are their custom will be lost for good; they will talk with their feet and go elsewhere!

You may work in an environment such as telesales, where the customer you speak to is a regular – but they may never speak to the same employee twice. Your contact with them will reinforce, or improve upon, a previous impression left by your colleagues. In this circumstance you can either improve on a great relationship or rescue a deteriorating one!

26. Develop long-term customer relationships

If you consider your colleagues to be your customers too – you may have thousands of long-term relationships to maintain! You may also be in a position that enables you to cultivate long-term relationships with your external customers.

In both of these cases it's often the little things you say and do that make the difference for your customers.

Carrie Cook's story is a delightful account describing a very special relationship that flourished and evolved over many months. She has shown that, more often than not, it's the little things that count in customer services.

Carrie's story

Flowering relationships!

Carrie, a horticultural assistant at Homebase in Finchley Road, London, was approached in the store one day by a group of three teachers and eight children. They asked her to help them choose suitable plants for their school gardening club. Eight children with special learning needs needed special attention - that's exactly what they got from Carrie. As Carrie took them around the various sections of the garden centre she used touch and texture to help the children understand and choose the right varieties of plant for their garden.

Carrie certainly made a tremendous impression on the children, as after a couple of weeks she received a lovely thank you letter and Christmas card. Carrie, wanting to return their compliment, asked Homebase if she could make up some 'Manor School Garden Club' badges for the children. With the full support of her manager the 'Homebase Manor School Garden Club' badges were created and dispatched to the school. The children were thrilled that their garden club had become so important!

As the relationship between Carrie and the school developed, she has received and accepted many invitations to visit their garden. In the spring, Homebase provided complimentary shrubs followed by free bedding plants in the summer. The original children have now moved on, yet the relationship continues. Each new class visits Carrie in store for the guided tour and, with the support of her manager, Carrie continues to provide the children with something much more than good customer service.

"A child can turn nothing at all into absolutely everything, and unhappiness to happiness."
Source Unknown

Like us, you will appreciate the unique circumstances surrounding Carrie's relationship with the Manor School Garden Club. You may never be in a position that allows you to develop a relationship with a group of very special children; however, you can experience the 'feel good factor' she enjoys! Carrie has numerous regular customers who seek her assistance; many of them are prepared to wait in line to speak to her! This is because Carrie, like Kieran, spends time fostering relationships with her customers.

27. The little extras for long-term relationships

As indicated by Carrie and Kieran's stories, in long-term relationships you can really get to know your customers well. The extra steps you take for customers cost very little, but generate great dividends. Long-term relationships give you the opportunity to consistently anticipate the needs of your customers. The better you get to know them, the more able you are to exceed their expectations.

The following is a list of ideas that will help your customer relationships grow.

- Invite your customer to call you by your first name.
- After asking their permission, call your customers by their first names.
- Obtain your regular customers' names and addresses, send them Christmas cards!
- Ring your customers regularly just to see how they are doing.
- Take an interest in your customers and their families.
- Make a note of any forthcoming holidays, birthdays and special events that your customer has planned. The next time you speak to them ask how everything went.
- Send personalised greetings cards.
- Invite them to special events or open days.
- Develop special offers for your regular customers.
- Send them free samples.
- Show them behind the scenes.
- Introduce them to the rest of the team.
- Send them regular discount vouchers.
- Send regular newsletters to your customers.

28. The proactive approach in relationship maintenance

Deborah Stewart, Trade Counter Supervisor, at RS Components, chooses a proactive approach with her customers. The implications of her relationship management are highlighted in her story below.

Deborah's story

Be proactive - not pushy

"We have a customer who orders large amounts of engineering resistors from us. While chatting to the production manager, I realised that they fed our resistors into a cardboard tube to aid the production process. I asked him for a sample of the tube they used and took it to our packaging department. I explained the customer's position to the team and asked if they could pack the resistors straight into tubes before despatch. The different departments do each other favours and they were happy to oblige both the customer and myself. When I contacted the customer and said that we could do this job for them, they were amazed. We managed to save them both time and money - at little cost to ourselves."

This relatively small, but significant, action showed the customer that Deborah takes a genuine interest in their business. She strives to do whatever she can for them. In terms of customer retention, the value gained from this type of personal service is priceless.

Don't wait for your customers to ask you for help – be proactive, approach them. Where appropriate make suggestions and present your customers with different opinions and ideas. If your customer declines your offer of help, ensure they are aware that you are available to help them whenever they need you. Remember there is a subtle difference between being pushy – and being proactive!

"A wise man will make more opportunities than he finds."
Francis Bacon

PICK UP YOUR PEN

Jot down at least five other things you could do to grow your customer relationships.

I could grow my customer relationships by:

THREE ACTIONS FOR YOU TO CONSIDER

1. Make a list of your customers and plan to give them a courtesy call on a regular basis.

2. Find out three things about your customers that are nothing to do with work, for example, their holidays, family events, interests and hobbies.

3. Ask your customers for an update on the above next time you speak to them. For example if they have been on holiday ask them what they enjoyed the most.

SECTION SUMMARY

- Establish a rapport with your customers and leave them with a positive impression.

- Put in the necessary groundwork to build strong relationships with your customers. Be friendly, invest time, listen, and empathise with your customers.

- Actively listen to your customers and channel your concentration onto each customer you deal with.

- Take advantage of the opportunities that exist to exceed the expectations of your long-term customers.

- Be proactive in your customer relationship maintenance.

"People of mediocre ability sometimes achieve outstanding success because they don't know when to quit. Most men succeed because they are determined to."
George Allen

POSITIVE ATTITUDES

29. Radiate positive signals

The expression on your face, the tone of your voice, your appearance, your manner and your behaviour all portray your attitude.

Positive attitudes are reflected in the uncomplicated things you can do everyday. A welcoming smile, an affable word, a real demonstration of interest, a shared joke, an empathetic glance and a genuine inquiry, are just a few of the small measures you can take that project a positive attitude. There is nothing mysterious about this approach; they are common sense strategies that will make a difference to your customers.

A positive attitude is also reflected in the way you deal with dilemmas presented to you by your customers. Do you concede defeat at the first hint of a problem or do you consider them challenges that you will able to overcome? Denise's story describes a whole host of predicaments that she happily overcame to satisfy the needs of her customer.

Denise Gould's story
Nothing is too much trouble

The corporate customers who are looked after by Denise Gould, a National Contract Manager for Guilbert UK Ltd, know she will do whatever it takes to keep them happy and satisfy their needs.

A classic example of Denise's premium service occurred

the day she received a telephone call from the area sales manager for Guilbert's Edinburgh office. One of Denise's corporate customers had, without any notice, arrived at the small Edinburgh site wanting to drop off five huge pallet loads of various goods. Not only was the site too small to accommodate the pallets – it was also up two flights of stairs! The manager didn't know how they were going to deal with the crisis.

Initially, to relieve the pressure from the Edinburgh site, Denise had the pallets redirected and delivered to the larger site at Livingston. From there she rang her customer and asked them exactly what their requirements were. It transpired that her customer had suddenly received an urgent job. Over two hundred and fifty individuals parcels, containing Post Graduate brochures for a fast track programme at a major bank, needed distributing. Some of the parcels contained hundreds of brochures to be delivered to Universities; others were to be delivered to the individuals who had requested them. Consequently, each parcel needed to be picked and packed to a specific order list. Denise's customer needed the logistical facilities Guilbert had to offer in order to complete their contract. The client assured Denise that, *"We knew you would do whatever it took to get the job done."* So they simply delivered the pallets of goods to their nearest office (Edinburgh), and left their bespoke order sheet!

Denise realised the importance of her challenge and recognised the significance of helping with the graduate recruitment. She immediately began to consider the options available to her. She was very much aware that if she pushed her clients order through the system then it would have a detrimental effect on other customer orders – the warehouse staff were extremely busy and simply couldn't spare the time at such short notice.

Denise realised that the only practical way of satisfying her customer's needs was for herself and another colleague, Suzanne, to *"Get our scruffs on,"* enter the warehouse, and pick and pack the parcels themselves. After a crash course in postage data input, Denise and Suzanne got back to basics! Five exhausting hours later they had successfully completed the task and had ensured the smooth and successful delivery of the customer's parcels.

**"For every obstacle there is a solution –
over, under, around and through."
Susan Alison**

In the scenario described above, Denise dealt with issues faced by her internal and external customers. She remained positive in her attitude and behaviour throughout the demanding period of time it took to satisfy the needs of her customer.

ASK YOURSELF

- How often do I portray a consistently positive attitude to my customers?
- How often do I smile at my customers?
- How do I sound when I answer the telephone – happy, angry, annoyed, indifferent or distracted?

30. Develop a positive attitude

Developing a positive attitude takes time and effort. You will need to be extremely self-aware and honest. Look deep inside yourself – treasure your positive attitudes and consider the negative.

Once you have acknowledged your attitudes about customers, and customer service, you must identify those that have negative connotations. This will enable you to address your negativity, reshape it and manage it more effectively. You can change your negative attitudes to positive ones. Below are three examples of commonly held negative thoughts, together with a positive replacement for each one.

NEGATIVE THOUGHT	POSITIVE THOUGHT
A lot of my customers are difficult to deal with.	It makes me feel great when I fix difficult problems.
My customers are always moaning.	I appreciate my customer's feedback.
My customers are ungrateful.	I am happy knowing I have done my best for my customers.

PICK UP YOUR PEN

Be honest with yourself and use the space provided to write down any negative thoughts you have had about your customers.

Negative thoughts I've had about my customers include:

Now replace these thought with positive alternatives. Write down your responses below.

Positive alternatives to my negative thoughts include:

Don't expect your thoughts to change overnight. A positive attitude is a habit developed over a period of time.

31. Be a positive beacon

The next time you experience a particularly busy day, go to the bathroom and look in a mirror – what do you see? Do you appear agitated, miserable or harassed? If the answer is yes, this is exactly what your customers see.

Become aware of the gestures you make. Your eyes, face and hands can reveal so much about your demeanour. Are you ever defensive, unfriendly, indifferent or dismissive? How often do you portray a negative attitude?

**"A clear understanding of negative emotions
dismisses them."
Vernon Howard**

---

32. Examine the signals you send out

Get into the habit of examining the signals you send out. This is the first thing a customer will notice about you. Think about it – have you ever looked for help in a store, or from a colleague, to find that whoever you approach is studiously avoiding your glance. We are sure that at some point, like us, you will have experienced the, *"I'm too busy to help you syndrome!"* Compare this attitude to the assistant or colleague that appears to sense your approach – they turn to meet you with a positive smile and a friendly greeting. You may have a brief wait for their assistance, however their smile and acknowledgement is enough to make you feel valued and content to wait.

**"Excellence is an art won by training and habituation.
We are what we repeatedly do.
Excellence, then, is not an act but a habit."
Aristotle**

---

33. It's your choice to be positive

Customers will move towards people they like and avoid those they dislike – it's human nature! *You* have a choice – you can get into the habit of being positive and draw your customers closer!

The next story is told by Andy Gilbert about a lady called Amma. In spite of personal challenges, Amma has made a choice – she chooses to be positive! Andy describes the amazing customer service she delivers.

Andy's story

Smiling through pain – being happy on the inside

I had arrived at Newark Airport, in New York, and now had to wait for nearly four hours until the departure of my transfer flight to North Carolina. Feeling a little thirsty, I made my way to the Presidents Lounge and ordered a drink. It was 19th August 2000 and a professional and friendly barman served me. As I continued to sit at the bar and read the book I had started on the first leg of my journey, I became aware that one of the bar staff had ended their shift and been replaced by another.

The new person serving drinks was Amma who was amazing in the way she provided great service to both the customers in the lounge and her colleagues. She seemed to have an ability to understand people, anticipate their needs and make them feel relaxed.

She was constantly aware of people who needed help or assistance. She gave them information, or asked them questions to enable them to make choices. When the needs of her customers were met, Amma turned her attention to helping her colleagues – supplying clean glasses; giving a newer member of the team tips on cleaning work surfaces - doing whatever she anticipated was necessary to help others. It was noticeable that she was a catalyst for creating a different, more uplifting, atmosphere for her team.

As she worked, with a constant smile on her face, she appeared not to be fully mobile and walked with a slight limp. We engaged in conversation and I mentioned how she appeared to enjoy her work. She commented, *"You have to like your job or else it ages you!"* She told me about her family background in Ghana and explained her beliefs were based on her mother's philosophy, *"Live the life you are meant to live; don't deceive people. Be happy; life is too short to be unhappy."*

As our conversation developed she mentioned the car accident she had two years previously and how half her body had suffered damage. Very factually, and always smiling, she described how she wears a permanent support belt, has regular injections in her spine and how her toes are still numb – two years after the crash!

I admired her ability to smile through her discomfort and give all her attention to the needs of others. Now, whenever I encounter people who are obviously unhappy in their job or cannot be bothered to care for their customers, I recall one of Amma's statements, *"I'm happy on the inside and therefore it's easy for me to be happy on the outside."*

34. See yourself in a positive light

Check your own self-image and attitudes. What kind of messages and signals do you give yourself?

Are you a negative self-talker? For example, do you say?

"I can't do...."
"I'm useless at...."
"I'll never manage that...."
"I'm so stupid...."

If you have found yourself saying these things to yourself, consider this: would you let a friend talk to you in this manner? Probably not – so why speak to yourself this way? Negative self-talk puts you at risk. The opinion you have of yourself is reflected in your attitude and behaviour. A negative opinion promotes a negative attitude – become positive and you will increase the probability of your success.

PICK UP YOUR PEN

Use the space below to write down the negative messages you have been giving yourself. Then formulate a positive message you will use to replace them with.

MY OLD NEGATIVE MESSAGES	THE NEW POSITIVE ME

**"You have the ability to leave a lasting impression in your own mind.
Make it a positive one; an enabling self-belief."
Andy Gilbert**

---

35. Are you happy on the inside?

Are you, like Amma, happy on the inside? If your answer is no, and you are at a time in your life when you do not feel particularly happy, you have a decision to make. You can either choose to mask the symptoms of your unhappiness and put your inner emotions and feelings to one side while you deal with your customers, or you could really make a difference to yourself by addressing the cause of your unhappiness.

"Different men seek after happiness in different ways and by different means and so make for themselves different modes of life and forms of government."
Aristotle

This book isn't the place to give you advice and assistance on making yourself happy. However, we have raised a valid and important point. Ask yourself this – how can you ever hope to exude positive signals all of the time, when deep down you feel negative?

**"There are two things to aim at in life:
to get what you want and, after that,
to positively enjoy it."**
Logan Pearsall

THREE ACTIONS FOR YOU TO CONSIDER

1. Next time someone asks you how you are say, *"excellent"* or *"brilliant"* rather than, *"okay"*, or *"not bad!"*

2. Only share the good stuff with your customers. For example, *"What a beautiful day,"* or *"I really enjoy challenges."*

3. Think of your worst customer and write a positive affirmation about them. For example, *"I really enjoy helping person X to solve his difficult problems."*

SECTION SUMMARY

• Radiate a positive attitude in all that you say and do.

• Remain positive in the face of adversity. Find the solution to every challenge you face.

• Look deep inside yourself. Treasure your positive attitudes and consider the negative ones – find positive replacements for your negative thoughts.

• Get into the habit of examining the signals you send out and make the choice to be positive.

• Check out your self-image and attitudes. Talk nicely to yourself.

BE SOLUTION FOCUSED –
THINK OF ALL YOUR POSSIBILITIES

36. How do you satisfy your customer's needs?

So far, we have established the importance of remaining positive when dealing with your customers. We have also discussed the significance of building a rapport and communicating effectively with customers to interpret their needs accurately. The next question to ask you is *how?* How will you satisfy your customer's needs?

In many circumstances, swift courteous service, delivered in a friendly and helpful manner will adequately satisfy your customer's needs. However, particularly tricky customer dilemmas, requests and requirements will demand that you stretch your abilities and imagination.

**"It's not the situation...
It's your reaction to the situation."
Bob Conklin**

---

37. Take ownership of your customer's requests

It is important that you take responsibility for all of your customer's requests and ensure that they are dealt with satisfactorily. Frontline ownership is a critical test of excellent customer service.

As a customer, how do you feel when you experience the following responses?

"You need to ask at the customer service desk..."
"I don't work in this department...."
"I need to speak to my manager about this...."
"There is nothing I can do...."

We imagine that, like us, you find these negative responses very frustrating.

ASK YOURSELF

- How readily do I shunt my customer onto the next person who may be able to help them?
- How often do I do everything in my power to satisfy my customer's needs?

You should aim to satisfy the needs of each customer who approaches you. Use your initiative and remain solution focused when faced with a challenge. Remember, each time you shunt a customer on to another person or department, their frustration and intolerance increases.

38. Achieve frontline ownership

Michelle, whose story is written below, takes control of her customer's requests. She has achieved frontline ownership.

Michelle Field's story

Not a problem!

Imagine you are a self-employed painter and decorator. You are working on the tail end of a big contract – and you've just run out of paint! Anxiety sets in; it was an end of range colour. You rush down to the local DIY store to buy more paint to finish what has become your nightmare job. You check the shelves – no paint! You find an assistant and hold your breath; do they have any more tins of the paint in stock?

Who would you rather have to help you? An assistant who replies, *"Nah, we've run out!"* or someone who replies, *"We're out of stock, but don't worry; let's see if I can track some down for you."* Of course you'd prefer the latter.

In her efforts to locate customer colour matches, Michelle Fields, DIY assistant at Homebase Livingston in Scotland, thinks nothing of contacting other stores and, in some cases, telephoning manufacturers on her customers behalf. The chances are you would leave the store knowing exactly where to go to pick up your tin of paint or safe in the knowledge that the paint would soon arrive safely in store following an internal stock transfer.

39. Don't pass on your customer's problems

Michelle's solution focused attitude certainly made a huge difference to the self-employed decorator who was able to complete his contract on time. What would it do for you? Michelle didn't shunt her customer towards the customer help desk; she wasn't defeated at the lack of paint in store. She considered all the options and came up with a solution that satisfied her customer's needs. Michelle has attitude – a solution focused attitude!

When faced with this type of challenge you need to think possibilities! What are the possible ways you could help your customer? Be creative – stay solution focused!

"It's not your position, it's your disposition."

PICK UP YOUR PEN

Read the following scenario.

Sue had purchased a variety of kitchen units from her local supplier. She was part way through putting together her new units when she realised that two particular components were missing. She gathered herself together, carefully folded her construction instructions, and made her way to the store in question. She entered the building and approached you! What are the possible things you could do to help her?

Write down, in the space provided, a list of things you could do to satisfy Sue's needs. Be creative!

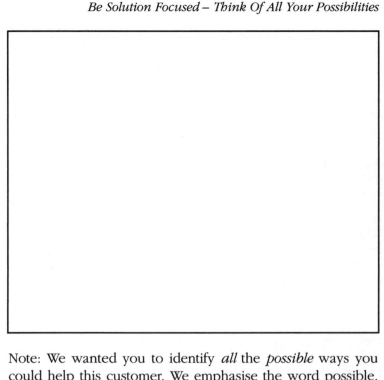

Note: We wanted you to identify *all* the *possible* ways you could help this customer. We emphasise the word possible. Make sure you consider all ideas and alternatives. At this stage it doesn't matter how achievable or practical you think they are; it's more critical that you consider all the possible options. Be solution focused – go back and think of at least four more ways you may be able to help Sue.

**"Nothing is impossible;
there are ways that lead to everything."
Francois de la Rochefoucauld**

---

40. Creative possibilities to help your customer

Donna Thompson, Team Manager at Royal and SunAlliance Health Care, needed to be very creative when responding to a desperate plea from one of her corporate clients.

Donna Thompson's story

Getting the injured home

At half past two on a Friday afternoon, Donna received a telephone call from the Director of one of her corporate customers. One of his employees had been involved in a serious road traffic accident. This dreadful event was further complicated by its location. The victim was stranded in a shabby medical centre, with very few facilities, in South America. His injuries were very serious and the medical care he was receiving was negligible.

Donna explained to us that in this circumstance Royal & SunAlliance's insurance cover would not come into full force until after the individual concerned was repatriated. Donna knew full well that the responsibility of getting the injured party home laid with her clients travel insurers. However, she recounted to us the desperation in the voice of her customer as he described the situation, *"I don't know what to do – I don't care how much it costs, I just want him back home. Can you help me?"* Rather than suggesting that her client contact his travel insurers, Donna set about doing whatever she could to satisfy her customer's needs. *"I told him that, I didn't know exactly what the next stage was, but if he gave me half an hour I would sort something out for him."*

After taking the responsibility off her customer's shoulders, Donna set about the task of bringing the man back to the UK. The first contact she made was with one of Royal & SunAlliance's medical advisors. *"I explained the chaps injuries to the medical advisor and explained the circumstances of the care he was receiving. She informed me that this was a grave situation that needed immediate attention. She also gave me the name and location of the nearest westernised clinic to where the man was located. By talking to her I had got a much better idea of what the man might be feeling and experiencing, and I fully understood his medical needs."* Donna immediately contacted the Director of the company and suggested that he contacted his travel insurers and insist that they transfer the injured party to the clinic her medical advisor had identified. This would ensure that he received adequate medical attention and he could be properly assessed to see if he was fit to travel home.

Armed with this information, Donna contacted a private hospital and asked about the possibility of them accepting a patient direct from the airport. However, she experienced all sorts of barriers to her request. The hospital was concerned about who would pay the costs of the medical care and the fact that a General Practitioner should refer patients. Feeling frustrated, Donna ended this phone call and contacted her Medical Advisor again to see if she had any contacts in the hospital. *"A friend of one of my contacts knew the Personal Assistant to an Orthopaedic Surgeon at the hospital. I got hold of the direct line phone number and contacted the surgeon's PA. After fully explaining the situation, and reassuring the hospital that any medical care would be covered by our insurance, the surgeon accepted our man as a patient."*

Donna contacted her client again. She gave him the contact details of the hospital, and surgeon, who were happy to accept responsibility for the injured man, just as soon as the travel insurers relinquished responsibility at the airport. In the interim the Company Director had already contacted his travel insurers, who were in the process of transferring his employee to the clinic suggested by Royal & SunAlliance.

Donna had gone over and above the call of duty in order to carry out the phenomenal task of organising this strategic operation. The injured party was air lifted by ambulance back to the UK where he was transferred to the private hospital organised by Donna. He has since made a full recovery.

Donna's actions that day made a significant difference to her customer. She chose not to refer her client to their travel insurers, but instead set about making sure Royal and SunAlliance did everything they could for them.

41. Accept the challenges you face

Like Michelle, Donna takes responsibility for all of her customer's requests. Donna's client telephoned her, not because it was Royal and SunAlliance's responsibility to get the injured man home, but because they had developed a strong working relationship with Donna. He trusted her judgement and felt able to call upon her for help and assistance. In this instance Donna acted as her customer's advocate. She considered all possible courses of action and worked efficiently to help her customer bring the victim home.

It would have been easy for Donna to shunt her customer on. In fact she was perfectly within her rights to suggest that he telephone his travel insurers (whose responsibility it was to make arrangements). However, Donna's solution focused attitude prompted her to accept the challenge presented to her and do all she could to satisfy her customer's needs.

42. Take personal responsibility for handling your customer's requests

As highlighted by Donna's story, occasionally you may be approached and asked to do something that may not necessarily be your responsibility or is outside your sphere of experience and influence. Nevertheless, you can take responsibility for handling the customer's request. For example, if you transfer a customer through to another department via the telephone, don't just put them on hold and redirect the call, check back on the line and make sure the telephone has been answered. If you are approached and asked to complete a task, about which you have no knowledge, don't simply say, *"I don't know how to do it"* or, *"I can't help you;"* help your customer locate somebody who can assist.

When you simply can't satisfy your customer's needs and you have to pass the responsibility for satisfaction onto another department or individual, get into the habit of checking that the customer has obtained satisfaction. It is up to you to take personal responsibility.

> **"Success on any major scale requires you to accept responsibility...in the final analysis, the one quality that all successful people have...is the ability to take on responsibility."**
> **Michael Korda**

THREE ACTIONS FOR YOU TO CONSIDER

1. Always tell your customers who you are and how to contact you.

2. Pause for breath, and then say, *"yes"* to your customers.

3. Eliminate the word *"try"* from your vocabulary – **just do it!**

SECTION SUMMARY

• Take ownership of your customer's requests. Ensure that your customer is dealt with satisfactorily and achieve frontline ownership.

• Consider all the possibilities available to help your customer.

• Accept any challenges you face and take personal responsibility for handling your customer's requests. When you have to pass on the responsibility for satisfaction to another colleague or department, check that your customer has obtained satisfaction.

BE PART OF A WINNING TEAM

43. Your internal customers

Are you part of a great service culture? Do you consider your colleagues and individuals from other departments to be your customers? Do you work together with your team to present a united front in customer care?

The response to these questions should be a resounding *yes*.

The degree of excellence achieved in external customer service is directly proportional to the quality of the internal customer service you and your organisation provide. You may be one of three or 30,000 employees. Whatever your circumstance you can make a difference to your external customers through the delivery of contagious internal customer care.

**"Every individual has a place to fill in the world and is important in some respect,
whether he chooses to be so or not."
Nathaniel Hawthorne**

---

44. Become part of the quest for customer satisfaction

Your internal actions have direct impacts. Jo's story, featured on the next page, identifies just one of many ways in which internal customer service can directly effect external care delivered.

Jo Hart's story

Internal customer service affects profits too

Imagine you're a customer and you want to purchase twelve specific components. You have looked through your supplier's catalogue and they only produce them in packets of ten. To get the number you want, you are going to have to spend £200 instead of £120! This seems a bit inflexible to you and you decide to ring your account manager to see what they can do.

How would you deal with this enquiry? The account manager in question was unsure of how to proceed, however he did feel able to telephone a colleague in the Marketing Department. The colleague he called was Jo Hart. Jo excels at internal customer service; he believes his colleagues are, *"Customers in their own right."* Jo has an open door policy - anyone can ask for advice, support or direction.

In this particular instance, Jo suggested sending the customer a complimentary pack of ten components. *"In real terms the cost to RS Components was approximately £30. This cost, when offset against the response of the customer, was negligible."*

The customer wasn't aware that the account manager had made the call to Jo and was delighted with the outcome of his inquiry. As a result of Jo's support and advice the account manager had far exceeded the customer's expectation. The customer proceeded to place a further £600 of orders with his account manager.

Jo's open door policy reflects his determination to provide first class customer care to any individuals that approach him. He provides a service that facilitates fantastic external customer care. In this particular instance Jo immersed himself in providing a solution for his internal customer that would consequently exceed the external customer's needs and expectations. Jo focused on long-term benefits for both of his customers, rather than short-term gains!

**"Dare to take an enlightened view –
it demands more, but the rewards are greater."
Source Unknown**

PICK UP YOUR PEN

Use the space below to identify just two of your internal customers. Once you have identified them, determine at least three ways in which you can help them to achieve excellence in external customer care.

I can help.................................by:

I can help.................................by:

Once again think big. Consider all the opportunities you have to communicate with your internal customers and all the possible ways you could help them deliver outstanding service to others.

45. Encourage team spirit

"Team – two or more persons working together."
Reader's Digest Oxford Complete Wordfinder

If you're self-employed you are a one-person operation. You alone are responsible for all aspects of your business. Your quality control should be first class - you are totally responsible for any customer care delivered.

If you're one of three employees, your team spirit is likely to be naturally strong. By this we mean that you will know each other well, you will work towards the same, or similar, goals and you will be aware of the quality of service provided by each team member.

"Team spirit – willingness to act as a member of a
group rather than as an individual."
Reader's Digest Oxford Complete Wordfinder

But what happens if you are one of thousands of employees? Then you must embrace your team and help bond it together. We have spoken at length about taking individual responsibility; it is equally important that you develop team responsiblity for delivering great customer service. Make your customer care contagious with the people in your team.

46. Work with your team

How many members are in the team you work in? A customer focused response to this question might be a figure representing the total number of individuals employed by your organisation. This mental representation may appear daunting, however it's a realistic response. If you concentrate on cementing relationships with those individuals you come across daily, your attitude will spread like ripples across a pond. Individuals working together, become departments working together, and departments working together ensure common priorities in customer care right across your organisation.

**"Remember the acorn –
mighty things from small beginnings grow."
Source Unknown**

You will read a story shortly that gives a clear picture of the point we are making. You too have the capability of starting a customer service revolution!

Kieran Dowling's story

A winning team

Guilbert UK Ltd were keen to improve productivity within their Transport Department. Kieran Dowling, a Transport Manager, was given the opportunity to explore the use of a bonus scheme to improve the productivity of his drivers.

Kieran was conscious of the impact that an individual bonus scheme could have on his drivers and was very much aware of the possible conflicts and arguments that might arise. For example, some drivers delivered on short runs and were able to deliver substantial amounts of parcels, while others had long haul runs with little opportunity to make multi-drop deliveries. Kieran was concerned that an individual bonus scheme would be unfair and detrimental to the dynamics of his team.

However, he did recognise and accept that there could be improvements in productivity and was pretty sure his drivers would like to earn extra money! So, he approached his team with a proposal. He suggested that the productivity bonus be pooled and shared out equally, with the understanding that several conditions were established. Firstly, he insisted that every driver left the warehouse at the same time each morning to commence their delivery runs. Secondly, when the drivers had finished their particular deliveries, they were to contact their colleagues and offer their assistance. Thirdly, each driver was to arrive back at the depot at the same time. With these guidelines in place each driver would receive an equal share of the productivity bonus. Not only was the proposal accepted by his team, it also had several positive, albeit unexpected, effects. Team spirit improved dramatically with each and every driver pulling their weight. They shared their skills and stamina, and productivity increased significantly!

In order for the drivers to further improve their productivity, help and support was required from the night sorters who picked and packed the parcels for the next day's delivery. The drivers quickly recognised the benefits the team approach had made to them and knew if they encouraged the night sorters to be part of their new alliance, the benefits would be even greater. The transport team volunteered that a percentage of their bonus should be allocated to the night sorters – whose productivity in turn began to increase. The night sorters not only earned extra money they also felt part of a winning team.

The effect of Kieran recognising the interdependencies between people doing the same job and the relationship between internal customers has been amazing. He now has a more productive team with high levels of mutual respect and morale.

47. Be contagious!

Kieran's proposal had several effects on the members of his immediate team. They became a more cohesive group, treating each other as customers as well as colleagues. Without further prompting on Kieran's part, the initiative spread to another department and team spirit and productivity increased further. This is a classic example of contagious customer care!

**"Contagious – likely to effect others
(*contagious enthusiasm*)."
Reader's Digest Oxford Complete Wordfinder**

ASK YOURSELF

- How can I spread my enthusiasm for customer care?
- How will I gain the 'buy in' and commitment of others?
- How will I involve my colleagues?

48. A customer service culture

We invited Bob Fitzsimmons, Claims Advisor Service Manager, at Royal and SunAlliance, to share his views on what it means to be involved in a customer service culture. Bob's genuine passion for customer care emanates from both his words and actions (an example of Bob's care is featured on page 29 of this book).

> Customer service is not something we do as a 9 to 5 and walk away. In many ways customer service is like a religion – you have to totally believe in what you do and understand why it is important to you. For me there are only two things that matter – the customer, and the people that work within the business. It is an absolute requirement to know and understand exactly what your customer needs, wants and expects from you. When you fully understand this you can set out to exceed their expectations. Delighting the customer is a must, and we must never stop looking for ways to improve our delivery. I have seen so many businesses fail or fall short of their goal. For many, the reasons were as plain as the writing on this paper. They never spoke to their customer and asked them what they wanted or needed – without this, customer service will fail.
>
> To achieve the level of service that your customers deserve you need to have the right people who believe in and understand what is being delivered to the customer. They must be empowered, inspired and have the tools to do the job properly. For the management team the people in the business are customers too. They must feel valued and appreciated for what they deliver for the customer. Now that we have our customers and our people totally immersed in a customer service

culture together, in partnership, then success of the highest order is guaranteed.

ASK YOURSELF

- How important is customer care to me?
- To what extent do I believe in customer care?
- How do I know what my customer needs?
- How do I know when my customer's needs are met?

"People are always blaming their circumstances for what they are. I don't believe in circumstances. The people who get on this world are the people who get up and look for the circumstances they want, and if they can't find them, they make them."
George Bernard Shaw

---

49. Start your own customer care revolution

The culture of the organisation you work in will affect your attitudes and actions. If you are fortunate, you will work within an environment similar to that described by Bob and be surrounded by attitudes that promote customer obsession!

However, you may be less fortunate. Your own personal values and attitudes may not be aligned with the organisation you work for – it's hard, but not impossible, to be customer obsessed if you're surrounded by negativity!

Remember the acorn? Mighty things from small beginnings grow.

You can still make a difference to your team. It will simply take more perseverance and creativity on your part. Change takes time and you won't alter the culture of your organisation overnight. However you can sow the seeds and begin to develop a sub-culture of customer obsession.

50. Creative initiatives in customer care

We have been working with Stamford Homes, a regional housebuilder, to implement a way of turning their culture into one infatuated with customer care. Every member of staff was invited to contribute to the formulation of six behavioural statements that, when used in a consistent manner, would improve the customer care they delivered.

All at the employees at Stamford Homes have ownership over these statements because of their direct involvement in their creation.

The Customer Care Culture of Stamford Homes:

We enjoy talking to people.
We care about what people say.
We seek to understand the needs of others.
We take personal responsibility to meet these needs.
We do what we say we are going to do.
We make people feel good.

These statements act as a company philosophy and a self-affirmation for each employee; they are applicable to both internal and external customers.

These six customer care statements have not only been incorporated on posters, leaflets and pocket cards but each employee is actively encouraged to make a difference by applying them and challenging those who don't. This initiative is both creative and effective. Stamford Homes is truly making a difference about customer care in the building industry.

PICK UP YOUR PEN

Your organisation may not have a culture so engrossed in customer care, but there is no reason why you can't become obsessed. Use the space below to develop six behavioural statements of your own. Then apply them in all contact you have with your internal and external customers and watch your behaviour become contagious.

My six behavioural statements are:

"A crank is a man with a new idea until it catches on."
Mark Twain

51. Customer obsession makes perfect business sense

We have included Sarah's story at the end of this chapter to accentuate the positive outcomes for customers when employees of an organisation work together as a team.

Sarah Partridge's story

Teamwork

Sarah, a Distribution Manager at Guilbert UK Ltd, knows how hard her sales colleagues work to secure orders for the company. She also knows how hard she and her team work to build on the first impressions the sales staff make.

Guilbert's sales team had been in negotiation with a petroleum company for some time, attempting to secure a contract for the printing and distribution of their in-store displays and pricing materials. Unfortunately for the petroleum company their existing logistics operation had let them down and they were desperate to get new pricing information and store displays countrywide by 10.00 a.m. the next day. They contacted the sales manager at Guilbert and asked if he could help. Conscious of how this may influence the outcome of the negotiations, the sales manager said he'd see what he could do. It was late in the afternoon when he contacted Sarah Partridge.

Sarah, realising the time restrictions in place (her working day had been due to finish shortly after she received the phone call), quickly began checking out the customer's requirements. She established that pricing information and numerical data from London together with further materials from the North East all needed bringing to the warehouse; the required information needed packaging into hundreds of parcels; and the parcels needed delivering – all within 24 hours! The customer's request was time critical following budgetary changes. The parcels contained new pricing symbols for the illuminated signs situated outside petrol stations – critical information to the public!

Despite the extremely tight deadlines, Sarah's response to the sales manager was, *"We'll do it,"* and then she set about working out how. She sent vans to London and the North East to collect the component parts, arranged overtime for some of her team and secured help from their couriers.

It was all hands on deck and by 9.30 p.m. the same evening 90% of the parcels were on the way to their destination. Sarah kept the remaining 10% in the warehouse for local delivery by her drivers the following morning.

Sarah not only helped out a colleague who needed a special service, she also made an important first impression to a potential new client who, on the basis of this service, awarded a contract to Guilbert UK.

ASK YOURSELF

- Why do I want to become customer obsessed?
- What initiatives will I develop to help spread customer obsession throughout my team?
- How will I change the culture of my organisation?

"The reasonable man adapts himself to the world; the unreasonable one persists in trying to adapt the world to himself. Therefore, all progress depends on the unreasonable man."
George Bernard Shaw

PICK UP YOUR PEN

After reading this section take the opportunity to make a note of any creative customer service initiatives already employed by your organisation, then list the creative initiatives taken for customers by yourself and your team, and finally list future creative initiatives you, and your team, could undertake for your customers.

Creative initiatives employed by my organisation.	
Creative initiatives employed by myself and my team.	
Creative initiatives myself and my team could employ in the future.	

THREE ACTIONS FOR YOU TO CONSIDER

1. Ask your internal customers, *"What can I do better?"* and share with them what would help you to do things better.

2. Arrange a team social outing to improve team morale and internal customer care.

3. At the end of this week ask your team three things:
   a)   What has gone well for us this week?
   b)   What has been troublesome for us this week?
   c)   How can we improve the situation?

SECTION SUMMARY

- Work with your team to provide a united front in customer care.

- Remember your internal customer. Never forget your internal actions have a direct impact on external customer care.

- Encourage team spirit and start a customer care revolution. Be contagious – spread excellence in customer care!

- Use and instigate creative initiatives in customer care. Get customer obsessed.

KEEPING PROMISES

52. Keep the promises you make to your customers

Keeping promises made to customers is an absolute necessity if you want to grow your business. If you let them down, you run the risk of letting them go.

In today's economy, it is the service you provide and the promises you make that gives you and your organisation the competitive edge. If you consistently break your service promises – you lose that edge.

- If you promise to deliver within twenty-four hours – you must deliver within twenty-four hours.

- If you promise to phone a customer back within an hour, you must phone back within the hour, even if it's just to give a progress update.

- If you promise to replace faulty goods without question, replace them.

Although keeping a promise made to your customer may appear to be a very basic principle, the surprising and frustrating fact is, many individuals and organisations fail to do so. Honouring your word must be a top priority – if you fail to deliver the goods and service you have promised, your own credibility is at stake.

ASK YOURSELF

- How happy am I to make promises to my customers?
- What promises do I make to my customers?
- What service promises does my organisation make?

"The more promises you and your team make, the more you keep and the better the service."
David Freemantle

---

53. Help keep your team promises

Can your customers depend upon the whole team and your organisation for excellent performance and response? Do you fulfil your commitments and help to keep promises made by your team? Steve Duff takes the promises his team make very seriously. The story featured next describes the extent to which he goes to fulfil his commitment as a store manager, in the pursuit of complete reliability.

Steve Duff's story

Keeping a promise and delivering on time

Steve, a Store Manager at Homebase Southampton Hedge End, believes strongly that Homebase should do everything in their power to honour the delivery dates given to their customers. A typical example of the measures Steve takes to ensure his customers goods are delivered on time, happened the day we interviewed him about his customer service values.

94

A gentleman had been quoted a delivery time of two weeks for a bath panel and the two week deadline was due to expire the next day. After checking the warehouse and distribution centre, Steve became aware that the panel wouldn't arrive in store until the following week. He considered this unacceptable; rather than telephone the customer and warn them of the delay, Steve telephoned all the Homebase stores, near and far, until he located a store that had the required goods in stock.

In this particular instance the Winchester branch had the bath panel in stock and Steve had arranged to pick the panel up on his way home later that day. The bath panel would then be in store the following day as promised. Steve's response to these situations is, *"It's not a difficult thing to do – you go to another store and get one. As far as I'm concerned if my team make a commitment and my customer expects their goods in two weeks, then that's exactly what they're going to get."*

Steve's attitude is undoubtedly customer focused. He also takes his position as an influential member of the team very seriously. He endeavours to satisfy his customer's expectations and, at the same time, sets a standard of service he expects from all of the team members. His role model behaviour and attitudes are contagious.

You may not be a store manager, but you are significant. You can set your own standards of customer care, and only you can decide if you keep the promises made to your customers.

"Hold yourself responsible for a higher standard than anyone else expects of you. Never excuse yourself."
Henry Ward Beecher

54. Make realistic promises

Ensure you make realistic promises; don't promise the earth and not deliver! Unrealistic promises lead to frustration, mistrust and dissatisfaction. Remember that you are responsible for the promises you make – promises made in haste are often repented at leisure.

55. Enhance your credibility

Customers will return to you if they believe you have credibility. Each time you, or your team, break a service promise your credibility slips. Customers will return to organisations they trust and believe in. They want security, integrity and the reassurance that if a problem does occur it will be dealt with promptly. Customers want to be free from risk and doubt and, as far as is humanly possible, they want to know their needs will be met.

"Credibility –
(i) the condition of being credible or believable.
(ii) reputation, status."
Reader's Digest Oxford Complete Wordfinder

At all times you should:

- Be true to your word.
- Do what you say you are going to do.
- Develop your reputation as a 'deliverer'.
- Be seen as a 'go to' person.

ASK YOURSELF

- Why is my credibility important to me?
- What do I do to maintain my credibility?
- How has my credibility been damaged before?
- What will I do to improve my credibility?

**"Undertake not what you cannot perform,
but be careful to keep your promises."
George Washington**

PICK UP YOUR PEN

What actions could you take that would improve your credibility? For example, you could make sure you meet every deadline you have set on behalf of your customers.

Actions I will take to improve my credibility include:

THREE ACTIONS FOR YOU TO DO

1. Always get back to your customers when you say you will, even if you have nothing to tell them.

2. Update your customers on a regular basis.

3. Once again, eliminate *try* from your language and commit to your customers – make service promises.

SECTION SUMMARY

- Honour your word – make sure you keep all the promises you, and your team, make to customers.

- Enhance your credibility in customer care. Make realistic promises; build a strong foundation of trust, integrity and security with the customer care you deliver.

SERVICE RECOVERY

56. When things go wrong

Occasionally things will go wrong and promises are broken. At some point you will have to deal with upset, disappointed and unhappy customers.

Sometimes problems will be a 'given' (outside of your control). For example, your delivery vehicle may be stuck in a traffic jam or, indeed, you may be stuck in a traffic jam – and running late for a meeting! Other instances might involve a mistake or miscalculation on your part. For example, you may have under-estimated the amount of time it would take you to complete a job, or recorded a clients order inaccurately. Occasionally your customer will misinform you or change their mind. However, you will need to take an active part in the service recovery and ensure their continued custom. Whatever the circumstance, you can make the situation better or worse. The way you handle service recovery will make a difference to your customer and, ultimately, your organisation.

57. What is service recovery?

Service recovery is the attitude and behaviours you employ when you are working to solve a customer problem. It's about the compensation and retention of customers. Each incident of service failure is different and will require a different level of your attention and commitment in the recovery process.

58. Make genuine apologies

For an aggrieved customer, a simple and genuine apology can often be the only thing needed to defuse a situation and prevent it escalating further. It costs you nothing to deliver, however the rewards can be substantial.

The sincerity with which you deliver a verbal apology will reflect your personal and professional concern at your customer's situation. Your apology doesn't automatically infer admission of guilt or responsibility – rather, it is an acknowledgement from you that your customer has been inconvenienced.

"Why is it that one of the most difficult admissions is I'm sorry?"

---

59. Little touches in service recovery

David Pitt, Call Centre Manager for Royal and SunAlliance, has found after many years experience that it is often the little touches in service recovery that can make the difference.

David's story

Sincerity is the key

The majority of David's customer contact involves internal employees. However, on occasion his expertise is called upon in matters of service recovery. A classic example of David's excellent customer care occurred the day he received a call from a customer who was extremely anxious. Despite paying his premium, the customer had not received a cover note for his car insurance. He was due to fly on holiday the next day and was planning on leaving his car at the airport for two weeks. He was understandably concerned about the service he had received and nervous at the thought of leaving his car unattended at the airport for a fortnight without adequate car insurance.

Following a telephone conversation, David took several measures to ensure the customer received a speedy service recovery.

David offered his sincere apologies on behalf of both his team and the organisation. He acknowledged the poor service the customer had received and promptly sent the documents by express courier to ensure it reached the customer before he and his family went on holiday. However, this wasn't the end of the story! David diarised the customer's holiday dates and made a note to call the family the day after they were due to return home.

On the same day David made the courtesy call, the family also received a bouquet of flowers as an additional token of sincere regret for any inconvenience they had endured as a direct result of Royal and SunAlliance's error.

David argues that it is these small touches that ensure the customers realise that Royal and SunAlliance value them; that they really care about their problems and want to work in partnership with them.

60. Empathise with your customers

When you empathise with your customers you are acknowledging and understanding their problem from their point of view. The most important thing you can do to fix any given situation is to listen to your customer. Allow them to air their views and, where necessary, let off some steam. By appreciating your customer's point of view you will be able to address their dilemmas in a timely fashion and offer appropriate recompense for their inconvenience.

"Many a man would rather have you hear his story than grant his request."
Lord Chesterfield

---

61. Be proactive in your service recovery

With today's technological advances, you have no excuse for not communicating with your customers. The telephone, e-mail, mobile phone, fax machine, courier, text message and pager ensures there is always a way for proactive communication.

Proactive communication can prevent a lot of wasted time and energy for both you and your customer. For instance, your customer won't be waiting for goods that are not going to turn up because of transport delays. Hence, at the end of the day, you won't have to deal with an angry and irate customer. Very often it isn't the lack of action that creates dissatisfaction, but the lack of communication.

> **"Proactive – creating or controlling a
> situation by taking the initiative."**
> **Reader's Digest Oxford Complete Wordfinder**

If you are running late for a meeting with a customer, be proactive and phone ahead. By telephoning and explaining your problem you will remain in control and can save your customer from a frustrating wait. This will defuse the situation; your delay will be understood! If you simply turn up late with no apology or prior warning then expect a problem; your customer will be understandably unhappy.

Responsive and effective communication is crucial in all aspects of customer care, especially in service recovery and circumstances described above.

> **"It's not what others do, or even our own mistakes
> that hurt us the most;
> it is our response to those things."**
> **Steven R. Covey**

62. Be honest with your customers

Every form of contact you have with a customer should be conducted in an honest and open manner. When things go amiss you should report the facts. Don't be tempted to become part of a blame culture – simply tell the truth. It could be that a message wasn't passed on, the wrong products were ordered, or you simply lost track of the time and forgot to do what you promised.

Your customer may have suffered a huge inconvenience because of your miscommunication or incompetence and the last thing they want is to hear a list of weak excuses.

What influences the customer is not necessarily the problem itself but the way you handle it.

63. Take steps to restore your customer's trust

For service recovery to be successful you need to restore your customer's trust in both yourself and your organisation. As we have already discussed, the first step along the road of recovery is honesty. Admit your mistakes and offer an apology. When the responsibility for the error lies at your feet, involve your customer in solving the problem. Ask them to tell you exactly how the issue has affected them and how you can help make things better. This will give back your customer a feeling of control and create a sense of partnership. Ultimately, reassure them that the problem is fixable and that *you* will personally make amends.

64. Offer timely resolutions to your customer's problems

After you have acknowledged your customer's problem it is important that you offer them a timely resolution. If you offer your customer an honest explanation for the failure to deliver adequate service, and demonstrate empathy and concern, you will find in most cases that they respond positively.

Customer's expectations of what will amount to a satisfactory recovery are based on many different variables. These range from their previous experiences with your organisation to the extent to which they feel they have been inconvenienced. The best way to ascertain what your customer will consider adequate recompense is to ask! You will often find that their expectations are a lot lower than the steps you would be prepared to take to recover the situation. This offers you a fantastic opportunity to exceed their expectations. Little things, when delivered sincerely, can readily compensate for your customer's inconvenience and distress.

"Bad situations provide the opportunity for great deeds."
Dee H. Groberg

---

65. Be creative in your service recovery

There will always be a way for you to make a difference to a dissatisfied customer. As we have already discussed, often a sincere apology and a honest explanation will restore faith in the services and goods you provide. In some circumstances a small gesture or token will prevent dissatisfaction. For example, many airlines hand out tokens to passengers of delayed flights, which entitles them to free food and refreshment while they wait for their scheduled flight. In other circumstances you must provide considerable compensation in order to limit the damage and inconvenience to your customer.

Paul, the contributor of the story featured on the following page, recounts a time when he went from feeling disappointed to being satisfied because of the measures taken to rectify a situation which occurred after he had purchased some new furniture.

Paul Broter's story

A perfect ending!

My wife and I purchased two sofas in a Christmas sale. They were a great bargain. We waited just one month for delivery of the sofas and when they arrived they were fantastic in every respect but one. The four matching scatter cushions that were part of our original order did not arrive. I telephoned the store and explained the situation to the customer care advisor who gave me a sincere apology and said that she would ensure the manufacturer sent them to us immediately.

A couple of days later the store manager telephoned to say that the sofas we purchased were actually part of a discontinued range. Consequently the manufacturers had no cushions available to send us and they had no material with which to make us a new set!

We were really disappointed. The manager's reaction to our dissatisfaction was great; he offered us several options to resolve the situation.

We could either have an immediate refund, the choice of a different suite, or some different scatter cushions made in a contrasting material.

Since we had grown to love our new sofas we went for the latter option. We chose some material and awaited our unique order! The manager assured us that in the event that we did not like the new cushions when they arrived he wouldn't hesitate to give us a full refund.

We were delighted with the outcome - the cushions were a perfect contrast! To top it all, rather than just provide us with the four cushions we had initially ordered, the store actually had eight made, providing us with four complimentary cushions. We have since recommended this company to several of our family and friends. Even when something went wrong, they more than made up for the mistake!

PICK UP YOUR PEN

Below is a list of three common service breakdown scenarios. After reading each one ask yourself the question, *"What could I do to make things right for this customer?"* Then make a note of your solutions in the space provided.

A customer's stereo equipment continues to have a persistent fault despite two visits to your service centre. The customer is frustrated and disappointed - not only have they been without their sound system for several weeks, but it has been returned to them in the same condition.

---

66. Benefit from your customer's complaints

The feedback you get from customers is arguably the most important information you will ever receive in customer service. If you deliver the service we describe in this book, we believe most of the feedback will consist of thanks and appreciation. However, inevitably things do, and will, go wrong over the course of your relationships with customers.

If you have built up a strong relationship with your customers you will be able to overcome these glitches. Like your own personal relationships, the relationships you have with customers can also go through 'sticky patches'. The important factor is how you deal with these potentially damaging times.

If a strong relationship exists with your customers, they will feel able to come to you with their concerns and complaints. If they can't come to you, they will vote with their feet and take their business elsewhere! If they can't take their business elsewhere (e.g. public sector) they will contribute to operational inefficiency through increased paperwork and beaurocratic processes.

Word of mouth is one of the most powerful forms of advertising Evidence exists that suggests a dissatisfied customer is far more likely to tell other people about poor service they may have received from you, than examples of outstanding service you deliver! This inescapable fact, combined with a poor customer relationship, will ensure that you and your organisation lose business or efficiency.

67. Turn customer complaints into customer opportunities

You should learn to treat any contact you have with complaining customers as opportunities. Learn from them; it's not for you to assign blame. Instead it's your responsibility to find out what happened, why things went wrong, what you can do to resolve the problem and, most importantly, what you can do to prevent it happening again.

In the event that you have to deliver customer feedback to other members of the team, present it in a positive, non-judgmental way. Use the information to grow your team and work out together how you can improve the service you all deliver. You have to achieve a balance between thanking the customer for delivering their feedback – even when it is less than complimentary – and reassuring and supporting your team so they continue to have the confidence to deliver excellent customer care in spite of any temporary setbacks. Good morale amongst the team is essential to maintain the customer service culture of your organisation.

"In the middle of difficulty lies opportunity."
Albert Einstein

---

68. Realise the value of your customer's feedback

We asked John Hay, Head of Customer Relations at Homebase, to contribute some of his thoughts about customer service, in particular his opinion of the value to be gained from customer feedback.

Customer service departments must be more proactive in dealing with customer communications, and learn to disseminate the information gathered in order to add real value throughout the business.

The examples highlighted throughout this book show that customer service is so much more than 'resigned behavioural compliance' (smiling at your customers!), and more genuinely about treating your customers as you would wish to be treated yourself.

All too often the word service is translated into complaints by businesses. Department Heads/Managers of many organisations see most of this type of negative feedback as a slight on their area, rather than positive criticism that can help develop and evolve the service they deliver, which in turn would result in a more efficient, customer-focused organisation.

Proper management of customer complaints and contacts should enable those in management positions to improve performance across the business, providing substantial returns on investment.

ASK YOURSELF

- How do I feel when a customer complains?
- What behaviours do I display when customers complain?
- How often do I ask my customers for feedback?
- What value do I gain from customer feedback?

69. Complaining customers are your best friends

Remember, a complaining customer is your best friend! They will provide you with information that will allow you to improve the service you deliver.

Don't be lulled into a false sense of security by lack of complaining customers. It is inevitable that things will go wrong – after all we are only human! If you don't receive complaints it doesn't necessarily mean your service is without reproach – it generally indicates that your customers don't feel it is worth their trouble complaining. Instead they will simply move their alliances to the enemy – your competition! It is important to ensure your customers feel they can approach you with their problems, you will then have the opportunity to make amends.

Your customers should feel that their opinion is important to you. Get into the habit of asking your customers for feedback. Ask them what you could do better; ask them what would make their experience more enjoyable; ask them what is the best and the worst thing about your organisation.

"Don't waste time placing blame; fix the cause!"
Zig Ziglar

THREE ACTIONS FOR YOU TO CONSIDER

1. Learn to say sorry.

2. Ask your customers what you can do to make amends.

3. Keep hold of your customer's problems, even if the solution is down to someone else. Follow up with your customer to ensure they have had a satisfactory conclusion.

SECTION SUMMARY

- Pay close attention to service recovery. The way you handle service recovery will make a difference to your customer and your organisation.

- In the event of poor service, make genuine and sincere apologies to your customers.

- Acknowledge your customer's inconvenience. Don't become part of a blame culture.

- Appreciate your customers point of view, address their dilemmas in a timely fashion and offer appropriate recompense for their inconvenience.

- Be proactive in your service recovery, communicate with your customers and at all times be honest. Don't present your customer with a list of weak excuses – do something and deal with their problems.

- Value customer feedback and turn customer complaints into customer opportunities.

"I am enough of an artist to draw freely
upon my imagination. Imagination is more
important than knowledge. Knowledge is
limited. Imagination encircles the world."
Albert Einstein

ONE CUSTOMER AT A TIME

70. Appreciate your customer's uniqueness

You, and your customers are unique. Your physical attributes, your appearance, your intellect, your humour, your attitudes and expectations all form your uniqueness. Even identical twins are distinctive in some ways; they have different experiences, different thoughts, different aims, different likes and dislikes. Recognising this uniqueness, and adapting your products and services accordingly, will enable you to deliver exceptional customer care.

"When we can stop judging and start appreciating people's differences, only then can we begin to learn from them."

---

71. Regard your customers holistically

Consider the following: if you were admitted to hospital to have, for example, your gall bladder removed, would you want to be regarded as patient No. 42 who is having a Cholesystectomy or treated as Alex, a 34 year old, who, despite being a confident business woman, is extremely anxious about her forthcoming surgery? Of course you'd prefer the latter. After all, you're not a swollen gall bladder; you're a human being with experiences, emotions, needs and fears – you would expect the medical staff to take these factors into account when preparing you for your surgery.

Medical staff are often cited as being the epitome of customer care. In a literal sense they do care for our physical and emotional needs. However, keep sight of the fact that you also care for people. You need to take into account more than just your customers' immediate requirements.

Consider your customers holistically. In other words, your customers are not simply Bob from Accounts, or A.N. Other who wants to purchase a dishwasher. They are complex individuals who have differing experiences, pressures and expectations. For example, Bob might be under extreme duress at work and desperate for help so he can prepare for a critical board meeting. A.N. Other might be a busy single mother who manages a hectic career and looks after four children at home. The dishwasher could be her most important buy of the year; it will almost certainly have a terrific impact on her time!

**"Do not wait for leaders;
do it alone, person to person."
Mother Teresa**

> **PICK UP YOUR PEN**

Imagine you have been given £20,000 to purchase a new car. Consider the needs, expectations and circumstances that will have a direct effect on the model of car you choose to buy. Make a note of your requirements in the box provided. Spend two minutes reflecting on your responses and consider your own uniqueness.

I would want my new car to have:

72. Flex your guidelines to accommodate your customer's uniqueness

Have you ever made a simple request as a customer and been rebuffed? We all have at sometime – Nicky, co-author of this book, will tell you about an experience she had.

Nicky's Story

When's a pint not a pint?

Wanting to take advantage of the fluctuating British weather I decided that I would take my son Samuel out for lunch one Sunday. We found ourselves a table on the patio and browsed through the menu. I had been to this particular pub many times before and enjoyed the variety of food they had available. It was a glorious summer afternoon and Sam and I were very hungry and thirsty. We quickly chose our food and I went to the appropriate counter to place our order. Along with the food I requested two pints of cola to quench our thirst.

Imagine my surprise when I was told, *"Sorry Madam we don't do pints of cola, only half pints!"* *"Oh, I see,"* was my response – *"well how about I pay for four, half pints of cola, and you put them into two pint glasses for me?"* After the pleasant young woman who served me recovered from my suggestion, I was even more flabbergasted to hear her say, *"Sorry we're not allowed, it only comes in half pint glasses."* I quickly realised I was fighting a losing battle, so smiling ever so sweetly I asked for four colas. The colas were quickly and efficiently poured with ice and lemon, and I ordered and paid for my food.

As a researcher and the co-author of this book, I am somewhat conscious of excellence in customer service. I decided that I really did need to make a point. However, this time I chose perhaps a more subtle but poignant way.

After thanking the lady for her assistance, I made one final request, *"Do you think you could let me have two empty pint glasses?"* *"Of course Madam,"* she replied. Yes, you guessed it! I thanked her once more then proceeded to pour my four colas into two pint glasses, passing the four empty glasses back to her. Her jaw dropped – and I made my point!

Despite the excellent food, my visit that lunchtime was marred by this small, blinkered action. I think I might try the pub in the next village next time I fancy eating out.

Does this scenario sound familiar? Rigid adherence to guidelines such as these makes for poor customer care. There was absolutely no logical reason why the waitress couldn't have met such a simple request. A lack of empowerment, creativity and initiative blemished what was once an untarnished reputation for excellent service.

73. Take responsibility for each customer

The customer service provided by Carrie Cook at Homebase is in direct contrast to the example given above. Carrie simply isn't a 'sorry, we don't do that' type of person.

Carrie's story

Meeting expectations

A lady came into her store one mid-summer afternoon and said she wanted two hanging baskets with her daughters favourite coloured flowers in them. This was followed by an explanation that her daughter had been in hospital for a long time with a very serious illness and that she was coming home that evening.

"Sorry, we don't do that," would have been an accurate response to this request, because Homebase do sell

plants and they do sell hanging baskets, but they don't normally make them up.

The customer didn't have the time or feel she had the skills to make a good job of the baskets. So, with the support of her manager, Carrie set about the task of making the baskets. Within 30 minutes the customer walked away thrilled with the baskets and with an impression that Homebase really care about their customers.

Carrie responded to a unique set of circumstances. She knew her customer's daughter was returning from hospital and that she was experiencing a range of emotions from relief to excitement. Carrie knew she could do something that would make her customer's life easier, so she did!

ASK YOURSELF

- What needs to happen in order for me to feel empowered enough to flex my organisation's guidelines?
- What can I do in order to make my customers feel as though they are being treated uniquely?
- How do I respond to the sometimes unusual requests of my customers?

**"All things are possible until they are proved
impossible – and even the impossible
may be only so as of now."**
Pearl S. Buck

---

74. Flex your organisational guidelines

Don't make the mistake of adhering rigidly to the system –
it doesn't matter how efficient it might be, sometimes it will
just not be appropriate. Occasionally, in order for you to
achieve excellent customer care, rules have to be
challenged, changed, and sometimes broken. Your routines
may have to be departed from and policies put to one side.

Margaret Scholan, a customer service representative at
Guilbert UK Ltd's Edinburgh office, often flexes her
organisation's standard practice in order to satisfy and
exceed her customer's needs.

Margaret's Story

Going beyond standard procedure

Margaret received a call from a customer desperate to get
hold of a specialist camera costing £3000. The customer
had been searching for this particular camera for some
considerable time. Guilbert was one of his last ports of
call. Not only was the customer desperate for the camera,
but he also required it within two days!

Margaret loves a challenge and, putting aside her initial
doubts, she made the decision that she was going to get
hold of the elusive camera. Not only that but she also set

herself the goal to exceed the customer's needs and obtain the camera within 24 hours! After promising to telephone the customer back, Margaret proceeded to dedicate her afternoon to the location and delivery of the required goods.

Her first step involved telephoning Guilbert's specialist request department and asking them for assistance in locating the camera - she made sure they also knew the camera was needed for the next day!

Margaret was delighted when, within two hours, she was contacted and told that the camera supplier had been located. However, it was at this point that she faced a challenge. Margaret was informed that it would take Guilbert five working days to get hold of the camera!

Faced with this daunting prospect, Margaret decided that this response simply wasn't good enough - so she asked for the telephone number of the suppliers.

Despite their initial protestations the specialist department, realising Margaret's determination, gave her the contact details. *"It didn't take much for me to persuade the suppliers how urgent the situation was. They suggested that I should fax my order directly to them as well as placing an order through Guilbert's standard procedure. I did what they suggested and the camera was delivered directly to my customer's doorstep by 10.30 a.m. the next morning."* Margaret's customer was absolutely delighted by the premium service she offered and the swift delivery of his goods. After days of fruitless searching, and only a few hours after contacting Margaret, he had in his hands a piece of specialist equipment he thought he would never obtain.

75. Maintain flexibility in customer care

Flexing the guidelines and treating each customer as an individual with unique needs and expectations may seem like extra work to you. However, the extra effort you put in has handsome rewards both for you and your organisation.

It shows your customers that you really care for them. By tailoring your products and services to your customers individual needs, they will feel both valued and understood.

Flexibility results in loyal customers. By treating each customer as a person, rather than a number or request, you make him or her feel special and cared for. They are significantly more likely to return for your special attention.

It gives you and your team greater confidence and pride. Your flexible and holistic approach will breed self-assurance, helping you to remain positive in both attitude and behaviours.

"If you follow all the rules you miss all the fun."
Katherine Hepburn

---

76. Make your customers feel special

Umang Panchal described for us his experience as a customer when he visited an Indian restaurant to celebrate a friend's birthday. His story highlights just how special flexible customer service can make your customers feel.

Umang Panchal's story

A great night out

If there was one thing I learnt while at University, it was that trying to arrange for a large group of friends to go out and enjoy themselves was a challenge. Someone would always be late getting dressed, no one would make a decision about where we were going (but everyone seemed to know where they didn't want to go!) and no one wanted to drive. And when it came to arranging to go out for someone's birthday the challenge seemed to increase ten-fold! I remember one such occasion in my final year.

We had booked a restaurant for eight o'clock and as usual we were running late. The group was not large – only six including myself. It was a small Indian restaurant called 'Geetanjali' just outside Wembley and had been highly recommended by one of our group. To add to our expectations, the whole group was made up of Indians and so we knew how good Indian food should taste! After we all got ready we headed off to the restaurant expecting to get a cold reception from the staff. After all, it was a busy Saturday night and we were already half an hour late. When we finally did arrive (at around nine o'clock!) we luckily got a table. We were seated by our waiter and then welcomed by a large bearded man. We assumed, from the expensive suit he was wearing and the authority he seemed to hold, he was the proprietor of the restaurant. There was no mention of the fact that we were late. The restaurant had a pleasant atmosphere and the customary Indian music was loud enough to be heard but didn't require you to shout to talk to someone across the table. We were handed our menus and we began the second phase of our challenge – finding food that everyone liked!

After we'd ordered our drinks the waiter came to take our food order. We all had our own particular requirements; some of us were vegetarian; some couldn't handle spicy hot food; some of us wanted extra chillies and the list went on! Sensing that we were struggling with our order, the restaurant owner came across to our table to help out. One of my friends found that none of the main dishes really appealed to him. The owner took charge and asked him what kind of food he liked. The restaurant owner listened attentively and suggested a chicken dish. There was no sense of inconvenience in his voice, only a sincere desire to create a dish that would suit my friend's particular taste buds.

While we were waiting for our starters to arrive we began to hand our cards and presents to the birthday girl. Again, the owner came to our table to enquire whose birthday it was and to wish them happy birthday. His genuine interest in his customers really came across. Throughout the meal the owner came to our table to make sure we were happy and that our food was okay.

As we were finishing our meal we noticed that we were the last customers in the restaurant. The restaurant staff worked quietly around us, at no point making us feel that we should hurry with our food. After we finished our meal and settled the bill we got our cameras out to take a photograph of the group. Again, without being prompted, the owner came to help us out. He suggested the best place for a picture and even asked one of the restaurant staff to lay a fresh tablecloth and take the photograph for us.

> Looking back at that night out, our expectations were exceeded. The owner and the staff took real pride in their restaurant. Their attention to detail added to the impressive atmosphere and food. The owner really made the customer feel king and took the challenge out of organising a night out with a group of friends.

The restaurant Umang and his friends chose to visit had been recommended to them by friends. This, when combined with their Indian heritage, ensured that their expectations were high. Following their experience at the restaurant, Umang's expectations were not only satisfied – but also exceeded. This group of six young people each became champions of the restaurant and the service it provides. It has since been recommended many times over!

"The measure of a man is not the number of his servants, but in the number of people he serves."
Paul D. Moody

---

77. Be the catalyst in excellent customer care

Who or what was the catalyst that triggered such excellent customer care in Umang's story? Rather than ask you to re-read Umang's story, we have listed some of the phrases he used to describe the experience he had.

"We were welcomed"
"Pleasant atmosphere"
"Sensing that we were struggling"
"Took charge for us"
"Listened attentively"

"Made suggestions"
"No sense of inconvenience"
"Enquired"
"Genuine interest"
"Without being prompted"

Once you have reflected on this list it will become obvious that 90% of the phrases are used to describe one individual – the restaurant owner! The food and atmosphere of the restaurant were good, however it is plain to see that it was the excellent care shown by the proprietor, that left Umang and his friends with such a pleasant memory of an evening out.

THREE ACTIONS FOR YOU TO CONSIDER

1. Ensure you are familiar with your company guidelines in customer care.

2. Ensure you are familiar with the products and services your organisation provides. Excellent product knowledge will increase your confidence.

3. Tell your customers how much you appreciate them.

SECTION SUMMARY

● Regard your customer holistically and flex your guidelines to accommodate their uniqueness.

● Don't make the mistake of adhering rigidly to your organisations guidelines. Become empowered!

● Remain flexible in your service delivery.

GENUINE CARE

78.   Add emotional value to your contact with customers

An organisation which relies solely on systems and processes to deliver the products and services it offers might be extremely efficient, but it will also run the risk of losing it's customers due to the lack of emotional connectivity it provides. You are the emotional aspect that makes the difference in customer care.

We have already determined that as a customer you would rather be treated as a human being than a number. You also know from your own experiences how it feels to be dealt with in a robotic and mechanised way. For example, the phrase 'have a nice day – please call again' is used by many organisations, but how many times on average do you think the person uttering the words actually means them?

79.   The importance of really caring

Barabara Henderson, Head of Customer Services at Guilbert UK Ltd, talks about service being a state of mind. In her contribution below she discusses how important it is that employees really care, and have a genuine desire to help their customers.

> Guilbert UK's major asset is the people who work for the company across the UK and Ireland. 'People' is the first word in our business philosophy, and the last. Our business....any business....is people. If we take care of our people, they will take care of business. Together we

harness their enthusiasm, experience and commitment with a common aim; to ensure our customers receive a service that exceeds their expectations.

We develop our people to truly realise their full potential and transfer ideas into practical business applications, which will enable us to continually improve our service offering to our customers.

Here at Guilbert we encourage our people to make a difference with actions that are taken daily. This in turn sets us apart from our competitors.

Our approach develops mutually beneficial relationships with our customers and enables us to work in partnership with each and every one. We aim to develop trust and confidence in our ability to deliver.

We strive to ensure that all our people, irrespective of the department they work in, believe in a customer service driven culture, and we recognise and acknowledge any individual who walks the extra mile.

Service is a state of mind – to give sensational service, our people must really care and they must have the desire to do it right, and do it now.

Customers are the sole purpose of our work at Guilbert. We want them to remain with us through choice and not through lack of alternatives. They are our passport to success; without them we are going nowhere. We believe that customer service is vitally important – satisfying customers is the difference between success and failure.

80. Develop genuine feelings for your customers

Many customer service personnel fall into the trap of delivering a programme of pre-set responses and behaviours. In most cases they are courteous, proficient and do the job sufficiently well. However, their service lacks the element that will bring the customers back for more – that genuine feeling of care.

Genuine warmth and concern is an almost intangible ingredient of customer care. However, it is quickly recognised and valued by customers. Within this section of the book we will share with you three stories that celebrate the care, concern, and altruistic acts shown in contagious customer care.

"Altruism – principle of living and acting for the good of others – altruistic...altruistically."
Collins Gem English Dictionary

Joy Wood's story

It's the extra things

Towards the end of the year 2000, I decided to have my kitchen refitted. I used a local company that some of my friends had used and I was very happy with their standard of workmanship and customer care.

The kitchen company I used had a good working relationship with a tiling company. I asked them to pass on my details to the tile company and was advised that Simon would be in touch shortly.

Sure enough, Simon contacted me within a couple of days and arranged to come and see me one evening. I must have been a rather unusual customer as not only did I want the walls tiling, but I also needed part of the floor tiling in order to complete a job that my husband (who had recently been killed in an accident) had started.

Simon was very sympathetic and helpful. He gave me some good advice over selecting the right tiles for the walls, was very patient and helpful about selecting colours and patterns. As I already had the tiles for the floor all he had to do was check that I had enough. Unfortunately there was one box too few to complete the job. He took a note of the batch number and style and ordered the extra tiles to save me the hassle.

Simon gave me estimates for both jobs and I arranged for the work to be completed.

I was very happy with the standard of workmanship and with Simon's attitude and helpfulness, but what really impressed me was the extra assistance that he gave me. Not only did he sort the floor for me, but he also showed me how to take the cupboard doors off and replace them. He also replaced a bit of skirting board for me that he had noticed was damaged and fixed my cooker door which was hanging off! He didn't have to do these extra things for me; he was just a genuinely nice guy helping a customer. I was very grateful.

"Caring is a powerful business advantage."
Scott Johnson

The little extras that Simon did for Joy showed her that he really cared. She described him as a genuine guy – as well as a skilled craftsman. Simon grabbed the opportunity to do several special things for Joy and in the process he added a lot of emotional value to his interactions with her.

ASK YOURSELF

- How much warmth and care do I demonstrate to my - customers?
- What could I do that would really make the difference to each individual customer I help?
- How many times have I gone out of my way to fix - problems that are bothering my customers?

Adding emotional value to all your interactions with customers is, without doubt, hard work. However, in many cases it is exceptionally rewarding.

81. Be sensitive to your customer's unspoken needs

Carrie Cook described a set of unique circumstances where she really had to use every ounce of sensitivity and understanding she could muster! Carrie needed to find a way of satisfying the needs her customer had not even expressed.

Carrie Cook's story

Customer obsession

An old man in a wheelchair, looking lost and confused in the houseplant section of Homebase, was the trigger for Carrie to step up and say, *"How can I help you?"* The old gentleman told her he had been looking for a 'Stephanotis' – it had been his late wife's favourite plant. He told Carrie how he had been widowed two years previously and that his wife's plant had just died. He wanted a replacement and mentioned that they only cost five pounds – they were cheap and cheerful and he could afford to buy a new plant.

Carrie talked to him for some time and identified that he was clearly still grieving for his wife. She offered to order the plant for him. However, despite her assurances that it was no trouble, he declined, saying he'd rather pop in each week to see if any had been delivered.

Carrie made sure some plants were ordered. However, when they arrived they were priced at ten pounds each. She put a couple of plants aside for him and talked to her manager about the customer. She felt that priced at ten pounds it would be a struggle for the customer to buy a plant. The manager suggested giving the plants to the gentleman. However, although Carrie thought this would be a nice gesture, she was concerned that he might be too proud to accept the plants as a gift.

Carrie came up with an idea. She waited for him to visit the store again and approached him with a Stephanosis, neatly labelled with a four ninety-nine-price tag! Carrie told us, *"Because he was so proud, I thought it was important that he didn't realise what I had done. He was so grateful that I had saved the plant for him and, to this day, he doesn't realise I halved its price. He went home a very happy and satisfied customer."*

In this particular circumstance Carrie provided much more than just excellent customer care. She had got to know her customer and genuinely cared about his needs. The gentleman concerned was thrilled with the attention and help Carrie gave him, even though he was unaware of the extra attention he had received. Carrie felt that it was in the best interest of her customer that he remained oblivious to the extra steps she had taken for him.

"In a flash of certainty, I saw that if one's motives are wrong, nothing could be right. It makes no difference whether you are a mailman, a hairdresser, an insurance salesman, and a housewife – whatever. As long as you feel you are serving others, you do the job well. When you are concerned only with helping yourself, you do it less well – a law as inexorable as gravity."
Arthur Gordon

---

82.   Generosity in customer care

You can be generous in so many ways. You can have generosity of spirit by being benevolent, humane, kindly, unselfish and humanitarian. You can be generous with your effort by being lavish, charitable, ungrudging and liberal. You can also be generous with your time. Occasionally you might also decide you can give your products and services freely. Acts of generosity come in many different guises.

ASK YOURSELF

- In what ways am I generous towards my customers?
- Why am I generous towards my customers?
- How does my generosity make me feel?

In many instances your generosity will cost you, and your organisation, nothing. However, the rewards will be great. You might be thinking, *"Ok – but what about the times when people give their commodities for free - that costs money!"* Our response to that is, yes it costs money, but you should look beyond that to the long-term benefits for you and your organisation.

We are not suggesting that you suddenly start distributing your goods and service indiscriminately. However, when the time is right and you feel this move is justified – don't hesitate! You may be in the position like Carrie, where you will need to clear your idea with a manager, or you may already hold the authority to take this step without fear of rebuke. Whatever your position there is always the possibility for generosity. Your actions will make a tangible difference to both you and your customers.

Generosity can be the prelude to considerable improvement for you and your team. Employee morale improves, satisfaction increases, environments become more positive and the 'feel good factor' is felt.

83. Restore your customer's faith

In the following paragraphs Debbie describes an act of generosity by a sales assistant that not only saved the day, but also restored her faith in customer care!

Debbie Gardner's story

Beyond the fondue

In April of this year I had my sister-in-law, Beverley, and her husband Greg, coming to visit for the weekend. As it was Greg's 50th birthday the following week I had decided to prepare a special celebratory meal for the Saturday evening. Being a fan of fondues, I decided on this and bought all the necessary food; mountains of red meat, sundries and copious amounts of red wine!

Come three o'clock on the Saturday afternoon, I decided it was time to start some preparation for the fondue and I went in search of my trusty fondue set. Having searched every kitchen cupboard, under the stairs and in the garage, I finally found it...in the garden! It had succumbed to the depths of neglect, being left outside for a period of six months full of oil and rancid meat.

By now it was three thirty in the afternoon, I had no fondue set and was running out of time. Following a brainwave, I decided to go to the huge designer outlet at Swindon and buy a new one. Although I knew the designer outlet was a forty-five minute drive away, I felt sure that I would locate the fondue set I needed.

My sister-in-law and I hastily made our way to the outlet and headed for several department stores. Our search proved to be fruitless. However, our final stop was a huge store that sold every make of crockery, cutlery, kitchen utensils, pots and pans you could imagine. Frantically we moved around the store looking for anything that resembled a fondue set. You guessed it – absolutely none were in sight!

Grabbing the nearest shop assistant, I asked if they had any in stock. She disappeared for a couple of minutes and then came back with the news, *"I am sorry Madam, we don't stock fondue sets."* Silence followed silence. I was desperate and my plans were going down the pan! At this point, her supervisor had walked over to join us. In a state of panic, I explained my predicament. Where on earth could I get a fondue set at 4:45 on a Saturday afternoon? The men were back at home preparing our food and we had nothing to cook it in! By the time I had driven anywhere else the shops would be closed.

Suddenly the supervisor asked us to hang on and disappeared. She was gone for a good ten minutes before she reappeared carrying a bag. With a big smile she handed it over and said quietly, *"This was a sample left by a sales company, will this do?"* Inside the bag was a Le Creuset fondue set. Now even to a novice like myself, I knew this was an expensive make. *"How much do I owe you?"* I asked, waiting for the bomb to drop. *"Oh that's ok, you can have it."* I thought she was joking, but she insisted that it had been sat at the back of the shop for months and since they didn't sell fondue sets I could have it.

Well to be completely frank I was absolutely astounded. I had never come across such an act of generosity before in a large department store. The meal was a resounding success and my faith was restored – big department stores do care!

The supervisor, who attended to Debbie's needs, considered her options, thought creatively and, in a moment of generosity, exceeded her customer's expectations. She also presented a very positive image to the shop assistant who was under her supervision. In her own way, the supervisor was spreading contagious customer care!

**"No act of kindness, no matter how small,
is ever wasted."
Aesop**

THREE ACTIONS FOR YOU TO CONSIDER

1. Ask your customers what is important to them.

2. Ask yourself, *"What is one thing I could do to make customers feel more valued?"*

3. Make a list of things you could do to make your internal customers feel more valued.

SECTION SUMMARY

● Add emotional value to the contact you have with your customers. Show them that you really care.

● Be sensitive to your customer's unspoken needs, and develop genuine feelings for your customers. Carry out acts of generosity while delivering customer care and restore your customer's faith!

● Remember an act of kindness, however small, is never wasted!

IT'S THE LITTLE THINGS THAT COUNT IN CUSTOMER CARE

84. The subtle differences

Attention to detail is critical in the delivery of contagious customer care. It is often the little things you do that will make the difference. A significant amount of satisfaction rests upon the ability of you to provide the extra touches that mean so much to customers.

Simple little things like picking up litter, straightening stock on shelves, emptying ashtrays, making sure information leaflets are available and providing magazines in a reception area, when added together have a huge impact on the impression you give your customer. They add up and go towards creating a pleasant memorable experience.

Paying attention to detail is hard work; you need to maintain a high level of vigilance. The very best way you can do this is to take a stroll through your system! Put on your customer's shoes and look through their eyes - evaluate the little things you do.

"The major contributory factor to any large success is the number of small, often unnoticed, differences made along the way."
Dr. Tina Welberg

---

85. Look for your customer care weak spots

Get into the habit of assessing the little things. Look for weak spots in the service you deliver. For example, you may have professional magazines in your reception area – but are they up to date or last years copies? If you record a voice mail message for your answer machine is it a friendly welcoming response or a brusque snappy, *"leave a message"?* These little things do make a difference.

Consider areas where customers may have to wait for your help – what could you do to make that wait less of a bind? Look for areas of both pride and embarrassment, and see what you can do to improve them. There are one hundred and one ways you can do the little extras that will make a difference to your customers experience of your organisation.

"Do what you can, with what you have, where you are."
Theodore Roosevelt

PICK UP YOUR PEN

Look around your environment. Identify weak spots in the service provided and make a note of the little things you could do to improve the situation.

I could improve service delivery by:

86. Consistency, consistency and consistency in customer care!

We have spoken about the importance of the little extras. The next thing to clarify is the importance of doing them repeatedly. For example, don't just have a clear out of your reception magazines every six months – get them delivered weekly! It will only take you a minute each day to change your voice mail message to one which gives a brief rundown of your whereabouts for the day. There is nothing more frustrating than continually getting the answer machine and having no idea when the person you are trying to contact will return!

**"A positive attitude is not a destination.
It is a way of life."**

Harriett Gilbert describes a tale of exceptional customer care that is made up of many special touches culminating in a fantastic customer experience. What's more, Harriett can guarantee that she will receive the same contagious customer care next time she visits Barrie Stephens Hair in Leicestershire!

Harriett's story

Groundhog Day!

Have you ever been faced with the dilemma, *"Shall I change my hairdresser?"* It was September 2000, following a house move. I had been to the same hairdresser for some years and, whilst she did a good job, travelling to her salon would take over an hour each way. I had spotted a salon in a neighbouring village – very modern looking – and I could see the stylists through the windows all dressed in black, some with wacky hairstyles. I became fascinated with this salon and each time I visited the village, I made sure I looked in.

One afternoon, after one of my frequent visits to the village, I was sat at my computer when an inner voice said, *"Go on pick the phone up and make an appointment."* So the deed was done, I had booked my appointment with a creative consultant; all I had to do now was turn up!

So with a few nerves, as well as some excitement, I opened the door to the modern salon with the people dressed in black. *"Hello Harriett, welcome to Barrie Stephens, Chantelle will be with you shortly,"* my welcomer said with a beaming smile on her face. My first thought was, *"Does this person know me from somewhere?"* but I didn't recognise her face. I was then shown to a seat and asked what refreshments I would like, which included the offer of a glass of wine. Other stylists in the salon seemed to take it in turn to momentarily stop what they were doing to either say, *"hello"* or smile at me. Then Chantelle, my creative stylist, welcomed me to the salon and talked me through the whole process she was going to undertake to create a new style for me.

Now I should mention at this stage that I worked as a shampoo girl before leaving school and I can remember checking with my client, *"Is the water alright for you?"* Having my hair washed by Chantelle was a quite different experience – not only were the chairs ergonomically right for the task, but Chantelle talked me through every step of the process telling me what shampoo and conditioner she was using.

Back in the styling chair, this very personal and thoughtful process continued, as Chantelle asked every conceivable question about my hair. Whilst we engaged in conversation, Barrie Stephens, the owner of the salon, welcomed me to the salon and enquired how I had heard of it. I have to admit I didn't tell him the full story!

All through my first visit I felt very special – it was almost as if I was the only client in the salon. However, that was not the case, the salon was very busy that day, and looking around at the other clients I got the feeling that they might be feeling special too.

Needless to say, with all the planning and preparation, my new hairstyle was a success and two of the other stylists, including Barrie, commented too. There was still more to come – after I paid my bill I was presented with a bag containing small gifts.

With my next appointment booked I couldn't wait to return to check out how good the customer care would be on my second visit.

If you have seen the film 'Groundhog Day', where everyday is the same as the last, that's just how it was. The same high level of customer care was demonstrated. Chantelle was excellent; she had remembered all of the conversation we had had four weeks ago and even though she had talked me through the whole process on my first visit, she did the same again.

I was now intrigued to learn more about how Barrie successfully manages this hairdressing business and Chantelle was only too willing to tell me. She explained that Barrie invests time and money for everyone in the salon to be trained not just with the skills and techniques to be a hair designer, but also about the way in which each of his team should behave with their clients. In fact in the short time that Chantelle has been doing my hair the salon has achieved the 'Investors in People' award.

I'm glad I picked the phone up and booked my first appointment. Having my hair styled at Barrie Stephen Hair has become a pleasurable experience, not a necessary chore!

"Do it big, do it right and do it with style."
Fred Astaire

PICK UP YOUR PEN

Identify five little extras that occurred in Harriett's story. How many of them can you adapt and incorporate in the service you provide?

> The little extras I can include in the service I provide are:

87. Deliver more than customer care

Royal & SunAlliance pride themselves on the consistent delivery of more than just insurance services. As an organisation they actively encourage the use of added extras; they seek to meet the needs of individuals and tailor their services appropriately.

Teresa Peace, a Team Manager at Royal & SunAlliance, unconsciously delivers an extraordinary amount of extras everyday of her working life. However, she doesn't consider them extras. For Teresa they are the necessary ingredients of outstanding customer care.

Teresa's story

Additional touches

Examples of Teresa's additional touches include:

- Asking customers when it would be appropriate to telephone them back, rather than giving them a time to expect a call. She is prepared to stay behind after work and come in early, in order to contact the customer at their convenience instead of her own.

- If through the course of her conversations with customers Teresa learns that, for example, they are about to get married (travel insurance for honeymooners is a real give-away) Teresa will send her customer a congratulations card from Royal & SunAlliance.

- She has sent flowers to customers as tokens of apology, sympathy and congratulation!

- She maintains contact with previously dissatisfied customers to ensure that they have no further problems with the service her team provides.

- She never uses the term 'it was a systems failure' as an explanation for service disappointment. Instead she takes the time to sort out the problem and communicates all of her findings with the customer – honesty being her policy!

- She has changed payment details, rather than cancel insurance policies, for customers who experience temporary financial difficulties.

These brief examples highlight the creative possibilities available for you to make a real difference. Don't just think about the possibilities available to you, commit to making them a priority in the customer care you provide.

"The only real way to differentiate yourself from the competition is through service."
Jonathan Tisch

THREE ACTIONS FOR YOU TO DO

1. Give compliments to your customers.

2. Acknowledge and say thank you for any superb customer service you receive.

3. Send a thank you card to a customer.

SECTION SUMMARY

● Look for your customer care weak spots. Identify how you can improve the service you deliver.

● Pay huge attention to little details in customer care. Ask your customers for their opinion and feedback and be consistent in the service you deliver.

● Deliver the little extras in the service you provide. Make the extras a necessary ingredient in the customer care you provide.

THE UNPREDICTABLE X FACTOR IN CUSTOMER CARE

88. The X factor

The X factor in customer service can be many things. It can be a pre-determined opinion your customer holds about the quality of products and services you provide. It could be a pre-conceived attitude about the service they expect to receive from you. It can also be something that is totally unconnected to anything remotely customer service orientated. For example, a personal crisis may have affected the mood of your customer which will have a direct impact on the interactions they have with you.

The X factor can be a help or a hindrance in customer care. For example, an individual may have received outstanding customer service from your organisation before and, as a consequence, have high expectations and anticipate outstanding customer care. On the other hand, they may have been told that your organisation has a poor track record in customer care and might be defensive or aggressive in their attitude towards you.

In either of these circumstances, it will be you that is on the receiving end of the customer's X factor. You have the opportunity to reinforce these attitudes and behaviours or, alternatively, you can make a difference by causing your customers to reassess their viewpoint.

**"Here is a simple but powerful rule:
Always give people more than they expect to get."
Nelson Boswell**

---

89. Change your customer's attitudes

You can help to repair any damage done to, and temper the disappointments experienced by, your customers. You can help restore your customers faith and break the myths associated with customer service.

Paul Roberts wrote the story featured next. It describes Paul's inbuilt mistrust of used car salesmen and how, over a number of interactions with a salesman named Richard, his attitudes and beliefs were transformed.

Paul's story

Would you buy a car from this man?

One Friday night in February of 1998, my wife Kath convinced me to drop her off in Nottingham city centre for what she described as a well-earned night out with the girls!

Together with my two-year-old son Owen, I drove Kath through the teeming nightlife to meet her friends. I had it all worked out - by the time I got home Owen would have finished his bedtime milk and be fast asleep. All I would have to do is put him to bed and, hey presto, my evening was free!

That week had been a particularly stressful one. I was under a lot of pressure at work and as I drove home I was busy contemplating all the work I would have to complete over the weekend to catch up on my schedule. All of a sudden there was a tremendous BANG and the car was shunted sideways across the road. I had pulled out of a junction and had not seen an oncoming vehicle.

If you have ever had an accident that has been a direct result of your ineptitude, you will know the horrible thoughts and feelings it generates. To make matters worse, my son was in the car. However, Owen was fine – he excitedly exclaimed, *"BANG! CRASH! Do it again Daddy!"*

Fortunately, whilst the car was severely damaged, with a little bit of modification (I put the wing in the boot), I was able to limp home. Later that night I sat there worrying. Kath had over sixty miles to travel to work everyday – she could neither work nor be paid if she didn't have a car.

The next morning I reported my accident to the car insurers, who were very nice. However, because the accident was my fault, I wasn't entitled to a courtesy car. They told me it would be approximately ten days before they made a decision about the viability of repairing the car. We were absolutely stuck. With a young family and a tight budget, hiring a car was something we could hardly afford to do.

Both Kath and I felt it was likely that the car would be written off. So rather than moping about the car we decided to spend the weekend getting a feel for the cost of a replacement car.

A friend of ours had recently bought a car from Carlton Car Centre and had commented on how nice the people were there. As it was nearby we decided to take a walk over. Like many people, I don't enjoy buying cars. I know very little about what makes a good second hand car and I have (or should I say had) an inbuilt mistrust of used car salesmen.

I was about to be pleasantly surprised! We walked around the forecourt for a few minutes and then a salesman, who introduced himself as Richard, approached us. I was immediately on the defensive, *"We are only looking,"* I said, hoping that he would leave us alone. However, he didn't walk away and, without being at all pushy, managed to get the whole sorry tale of my misadventure from me.

What he did next changed my impression of car salesmen forever. Knowing that we may not need a replacement car (remember at this point we didn't know for sure that our car would be written off), he offered to loan us a car free of charge until the insurers reached their decision. He made it clear that we had no obligation to buy the car from him after this period. The cynical sceptic inside of me was screaming, *"Why, What's the catch?"* But there wasn't one!

Obviously Richard could see the potential of the sale, but there was no guarantee we would eventually buy a car from him. He asked us what kind of car we would like and for an approximate idea of the price we would seek to pay. I have to be honest I still couldn't quite believe it. However, Kath and I drove away in a Rover car, on loan, free of charge!

Two weeks later the insurance company wrote the car off and posted me a cheque.

Because of the service we had received, we decided to return to Richard to see what he had available. We were stunned - not only had he given the car to us for two weeks free of charge, he had also made it his business to look around for a car of the type we were looking for.

Although it was two hundred pounds more than our budget allowed, after a friendly haggle Richard reduced the asking price by one hundred and fifty pounds.

Since that purchase I have recommended Carlton Car Centre many times. My father bought his next car from Richard, as did a close friend of mine. Recently Kath and I purchased a second car from Richard too.

Would I buy a used car from this man? – The answer is YES, YES and YES!

90. Match the goods and services you provide to each individual customer

Richard provides excellent customer care. He finds out what his customers really need, what they would really like and how much money they have to spend. Then he simply matches the service and products he provides to each individual customer!

Richard's outstanding service changed Paul's attitude. For the first time he was faced with a man who totally contradicted every belief he had formulated about used car sales. Richard appreciated the uniqueness of Paul's situation and the implications this had on his life.

> **"A kind and compassionate act is**
> **often it's own reward."**
> **William J. Bennett**

PICK UP YOUR PEN

Cast your mind back and think of a situation where you had to deal with a customer who displayed a negative attitude towards you. What would you do differently if you came across them again?

Things I would do differently include:

91. Your unpredictable X factor

We all have the occasional bad day – in fact some of them are appalling! There will be occasions where the last thing you want to do is put on a brave face and smile. However, when providing contagious customer care you cannot let your negative moods affect others. If you really want to deliver fantastic customer care you will have to learn to leave your troubles behind when you enter your working environment.

The image you present to your customers should be consistently positive and friendly. Your customers really don't care if you had very little sleep the night before; if a relative of yours is poorly; or if you had an argument with your partner minutes before you left the house that morning. They have come to you for the services or products you provide and they certainly won't excuse any negative or rude behaviour on your part.

92. Reap what you sow!

On the days when all is not well with you, as soon as you enter your place of work endeavour to make a conscious decision to portray a positive image. Smile, even if you don't feel like it. If somebody asks how you are, reply with 'great' or 'fantastic' even if you feel tired and defeated. You need to help yourself as well as helping others.

Develop a positive self-affirmation – get used to telling yourself how marvellous you are, how glad you are to be alive, remind yourself of the many small differences you will make that day and how much you enjoy serving your customers.

> **"Take care that the face that looks out from the mirror in the morning is a pleasant face. You may not see it again during the day, but others will."**
> **Source Unknown**

Your mind is a fertile place, if you think positive - you will be positive; think negative and you will be negative. Remember, **you** can choose what **you** think and **you** will reap what **you** sow – it therefore makes sense to sow positive thoughts!

ASK YOURSELF

- How often do I smile and welcome my customers even if I'm in a bad mood?
- How effective am I at leaving my personal troubles at home?
- What do I do when I recognise that I'm feeling fed up and stressed?

93. Dealing with angry customers

It is clear that it's helpful to leave your negative moods and behaviours behind when dealing with a customer. However, don't expect your customers to do the same for you! The personal experiences they have will influence the attitudes and behaviours they show you. Customers are people and occasionally they will be angry, offensive and down-right rude. You don't have to work in a complaints department to catch this type of flack from irate customers – it simply comes with the service territory!

What the customer is upset about may not be anything to do with you – but he/she doesn't care about that – they are just upset and you're the person who is closest to hand.

We don't suggest that you put up with abuse. There may be occasions when you have to call in reinforcements and firmly tell the customer that you will end the conversation if the tirade doesn't cease. However, there are steps you can take to alleviate the situation and, in some circumstances, make your customer's day so much better!

- React in a helpful manner. A defensive attitude will only prompt further abuse, while a friendly helpful manner will, to a certain extent, disarm the irate customer.

- Keep your cool! Never allow a customer to put you on the defensive. This is a lose – lose situation. If you argue back with your customers, one of two situations will arise: either you will make them look foolish or you will allow them to make you look foolish. Either way, the chances are you will lose them as a customer.

- Don't take things personally. Angry and upset people often say things they don't mean in the heat of the moment.

- If the customer has a problem with products and services provided by your organisation, tell your customer what you're going to do to solve their dilemma – and then do it!

"If you're right there is no reason to lose your temper. If you're wrong, you can't afford to lose it."
Source Unknown

---

94. Make your customer feel better

There will be occasions when you can make a difference to your customers just by being kind and thoughtful if they are having a bad day! They may be sad, embarrassed, ashamed or insecure; whatever their circumstances don't underestimate what a friendly face and a smile can do to brighten your customers day.

Steve Duff, Store Manager at Southampton Hedge End Homebase store, often takes measures to try and improve his customer's day.

Steve's story

It's no use crying over spilt paint!

You've just bought a five-litre tin of bright red paint from your local Homebase store. You're loading your purchases into the boot of your car when the worst happens. Despite being careful to store the tin in an upright position – you were distracted for just a second – you've now got red paint running all over your boot space!

How would you feel? This sticky situation actually happened in the car park of a branch of Homebase managed by Steve. Although the company is not responsible for goods once they have left the store, Steve always goes beyond the call of duty to do what he can for his customers. He rolled up his shirtsleeves, grabbed a bucket of water and cleaning solution, and helped the distraught customer to scrub the paint off the floor of the car. Once the customer (and the carpet) had recovered, Steve then replaced the offending article free of charge and ensured it was safely secured for the journey home. While not being a perfect end to a shopping trip, Steve went along way towards restoring his customer's sanity and spilt paint!

Can you imagine how the customer felt? There was no need for Steve to take these steps for his customer. However, in doing so he delivered outstanding customer care in a benevolent and friendly manner. Steve knew he had the ability to make the customer feel better – so he did.

"Spread a little happiness as you go by."
Vivienne Ellis

---

95. If your customer is having a bad day

Kath Fawcett describes a 'gem' of a man who displayed real kindness to her at a time when she felt particularly silly!

Kath's story

A knight in a shiny RAC van!

One autumn I left work in a bit of a rush. I was due to pick up my son from nursery and was cutting it fine for the 45 minute journey before the nursery shut at 6 o'clock.

I was on track until I was about ten miles from the office and thirty minutes from home. There was a sign "ROAD CLOSED – FLOOD". I felt my stomach sink, if I took the detour I wasn't going to make it home in time. I knew that stretch of road well and there had been a few times in the past when I actually negotiated the floodwater. I

161

sat, waited and watched. I saw half a dozen cars go through, many of them smaller than mine. Yes the water did look deeper than normal but if they could do it so could I!

I set off following the path of another car, which as it turns out may have been my downfall. About half way through the floods, yes, you've guessed it, my car coughed, spluttered and died on me. I turned the key – nothing. I turned the key again, with my foot on the accelerator – nothing. So there I was stuck in about eighteen inches of water. Nothing for it but to get out and push. In the freezing cold water up to my knees I managed to push my little car to dry land.

I tried to start the engine again without any luck and even a passing mechanic had a go! He decided that the water had managed to completely seize up my engine. Standing there in sopping wet trousers and shoes I made the call to the RAC control centre and was told that someone would be with me as soon as possible. I also contacted my neighbours and asked them to pick up my son.

Feeling miserable, cold and worried I sat and waited. At this stage I was also starting to feel a bit stupid for having ignored the road closed signs and about the resulting damage to my car. Twenty minutes later the RAC van was in sight.

John, my rescuer, introduced himself and his first concern was how cold and wet I was. By this stage my teeth were chattering and I was cold all over. He got me into his van, put the heater on full blast and talked to me about what had happened. Having looked at the car he established there was no way it could be fixed at the roadside. That meant that both the car and myself would need to be transported home. This entailed a bit of a wait as John needed to call out a contractor with towing equipment.

Strictly speaking, John should have left me and moved onto his next job. However, he was concerned about me being left by myself, particularly because I would have to sit in a car with no heating. He rang into the control centre, explained the situation in detail and made it clear that he was going to stop with me until the recovery vehicle arrived. On hearing John's side of the conversation I got the impression that the control centre would rather John had moved onto his next job. However, he was insistent that I couldn't be left alone. John was treating me as an individual and was concerned about my personal welfare.

He then set about getting me as warm as possible, supplying me with blankets and leaving the heating on full. As I expected it was a long wait. John shared his liquorish allsorts with me (it was well past tea-time!) and he passed the time by taking an interest in my work and my family. But what made John's customer service exceptional was how he helped me to realise that what had happened was just one of those things and I wasn't stupid.

He never asked once why I had chosen to go through the floodwater. Instead he talked about how it was just a fluke, how it could of happened to anyone and that it was just bad luck. He pointed out that other cars had made it through and there was no reason why mine couldn't have done the same.

> After ninety minutes of waiting, the recovery vehicle arrived and it was time to say goodbye to John. He was someone who had taken a genuine interest in me and had taken the time to build a personal relationship even though he was unlikely to ever meet me again. He made sure everything was okay and that I would be able to get home safely before he left. So many thanks to John, not just for his personal touch, warmth and food but also the kindness he displayed in sparing my feelings over my flood escapade!

Being kind to customers costs you nothing and yet it can mean so much. The kindness shown to Kath made her feel better about herself and the situation she had found herself in. The next time you are approached by a disgruntled customer, treat them as you would an unhappy friend. You will be surprised at the difference it makes.

ASK YOURSELF

- What do I do to make my customers feel good about themselves?
- In my everyday dealings with customers how often do I consider what kind of day they have had?
- How do I know what kind of mood or frame of mind my customer is in?

**"A healthy attitude is contagious, but don't wait to
catch it from others – be a carrier!"
Source Unknown**

THREE ACTIONS FOR YOU TO CONSIDER

1. Don't take your customer's bad moods personally.

2. Treat your angry customers with kindness and helpfuness.

3. Don't pre-judge your customers.

- Be aware of your X factor! Always be prepared for the unexpected.

- Match the services and goods you provide to meet the needs of individual customers. Influence their behaviour with your attitude.

- Your mind is a fertile place. Make sure you sow positive thoughts and attitudes – remember you will reap what you sow.

- Keep cool when dealing with angry customers. Tell customers what you are going to do to solve their dilemma – then do it!

- Spread a little happiness and make your customer feel better – remember your customer has a X factor too.

SOME FINAL THOUGHTS

96. Everybody has a part to play – including you!

As you have been reading this book, there may have been times when you thought, *"this is all well and good but it doesn't really apply to me."* Well stop right there; we are here to tell you *yes* it does apply to you. Everybody has his or her part to play in contagious customer care. You may be a company director, a shop assistant or an office cleaner; it doesn't matter what role or job title you have – at some point you will have contact with either internal or external customers. You can apply all of the hints and tips we have discussed in this book, irrespective of your position. All you need is the right attitude!

97. Common sense in customer care

There is nothing magical about customer service. A majority of the differences you can make are based on good old-fashioned common sense. If you are prepared to turn common sense into common practice you will become part of the contagious customer care revolution. You will make a huge difference to yourself, your customers and your organisation.

"Common sense in an uncommon degree is what the world calls wisdom."
Samuel Taylor Coleridge

---

98.   Use your initiative in customer care

We couldn't possibly cover all of the material available on customer service in one book. What we have provided you with is a book packed full of practical tips and ideas followed by inspirational stories, which highlight the points we are making.

We encourage you to use your initiative in customer service and do what the people featured in this book have done. Do what you know is right, in the best way you know how.

99.   Everyone can make a difference

We are here to tell you that everybody can make a difference in customer care. The last two stories featured in this book are told by Paul Jackson of RS Components and they highlight the part everyone has to play in the customer service image presented by organisations.

Paul's story

Everyone can make a difference

A night security guard became the hero of the hour, long before a company's twenty-four hour service became available.

After experiencing a major breakdown, engineers from a North Sea oil rig were in desperate need of a replacement component. None were available to them locally and thousands of pounds of revenue were being lost for every hour the rig couldn't pump oil. The engineers involved decided to charter a helicopter and fly to their suppliers, RS Components, in the middle of the night. Bearing in mind that this supplier had not yet implemented twenty-four hour customer service, some might say that this was rather a rash move. However, despite the unsociable hour, the engineers obviously felt confident that they would get the help they needed.

Put yourself in the position of the night security guard. Would you have been able to help? Imagine a helicopter, not to mention some pretty harassed engineers, descending in the early hours of the morning. When they arrive you've never heard of the part they want – let alone know where it's stored! Would you have the nerve to throw open the doors of the company warehouse? That's exactly what the guard did. Without the use of a computer, or any other help, the security guard scoured the massive warehouse and eventually located the required part. Without any fuss or requirements for bureaucratic paperwork, the guard handed the part over and the helicopter took off. Within a few short hours the rig was pumping oil again.

The guard Paul told us about in this story used his initiative and common sense. He recognised that the customer was in serious trouble, and he had a way of providing a solution to their problem.

This certainly wasn't part of the guard's job description – the most activity he normally came across on the night shift was the odd urban fox and courting couple! However, it just goes to show that with the right attitude, plenty of common sense and a little creative initiative you too could satisfy your customer's needs.

> **"A creative attitude is the fuel of
> progress and growth."
> Source Unknown**

100. The ultimate opportunity

Although small opportunities to help others happen on a
daily basis, we are privileged if we can become part of an
occasion that can help save a life.

Paul was keen to share this last story with us as he felt very
fortunate to have been able to take part in making such a
huge difference to one particularly small customer.

Customer service saves a life!

Emotions ran high the day RS Components received a
call from Kettering General hospital, urgently requesting
a replacement component for an incubator. The
incubator was needed to transfer a critically ill newborn
baby to a specialist neurological unit in Oxford.

Paul Jackson described the atmosphere in the call centre
that day, *"Everything stopped. This request transcended
all normal services; it was obviously an emergency and
had to be dealt with immediately."* Can you imagine
being in a position where wasted seconds are more like
wasted hours? Where accuracy and speed are of
paramount importance? When satisfying a need can help
save a life?

Imagine the scenario. A group of men and women, many
of them parents, are suddenly plunged into a position of

huge responsibility – the atmosphere is electric – the normal level of activity increases tenfold. Everyone pulls together, each individual aware that their input is crucial. Absolutely no mistakes can be made – the consequences of an error would be fatal.

The majority of calls into the centre that day were taken by a minority of the staff. This freed a team dedicated to satisfying the request made by the hospital.

While nurses, doctors and ambulance crews waited anxiously for news, the team at RS Components went to work. Acutely aware of the tiny baby that was holding onto life by a thread, they concentrated on the task at hand, the team worked as if they were one. *"We picked, packed and couriered the replacement part in record time. Literally everybody in the call centre made this possible."*

The team at RS Components pulled out all the stops; with absolute focus they delivered faultless customer care. The difference they made that day was life saving. *"We got a letter back saying that if they had transferred the baby to Oxford without the support of the incubator, then it's quite likely that the baby wouldn't have survived."*

The memory of that day will stay forever etched on the memories of those involved. The evidence of their dedication and superior service lives on in the best possible way – a happy and healthy addition to the human race.

You may never be in the position to take part in such a phenomenal act of customer service; however, you may already being doing so, possibly without realising it!

The important thing is for you to make a difference – large or small. Take heed, take heart and take action!

"There is little difference in people, but that little difference makes a big difference. The little difference is attitude. The big difference is whether it is positive or negative."
W. Clement Stone

SECTION SUMMARY

- You are important, and you do make a difference. Everybody has a part to play in customer care.

- Use plenty of common sense in customer care. Turn common sense into common practice.

- Use your initiative in the service you provide. If something feels right – do it!

YOU'VE READ THE BOOK –
SO WHAT NEXT?

101. What next?

We wrote this book in the hope that you will choose to make a difference and deliver contagious customer care. It's up to you now – we've done our bit! Only you can choose to apply the learning you have encountered in this book. The following quote is one that is often used in our organisation. It was taken from an interview we carried out with a successful individual as part of the original Go MAD® research.

**"The difference between those that do
and those that don't,
is those that are prepared to have a go.
And really have a go, despite the obstacles."
Simon Ashton.**

Are you prepared to have a go – a *real* go? If not, take at least one contagious step and pass this book onto someone who really does want to make a difference in customer care.

102. Find the learning points that relate to you

Each section of the book ends with a summary of learning points. These learning points can be easily accessed by referring to the pages below. Use them to consolidate the information given in each individual chapter.

103.   Index of stories

The 29 case-studies and stories we have used in this book are indexed below. Feel free to browse the list and see which ones grab your attention. You can choose to go straight to those that interest you and enjoy the inspirational message they tell.

104. The future

In future books we will be including further letters and stories about contagious customer care.

You can become involved and provide inspiration to others by writing to us and sharing your stories about fantastic customer care. Whether you are a service employee or a customer we would love to hear from you.

Our mailing address is:

Go MAD Books
Pocket Gate Farm
Off Breakback Road
Woodhouse Eaves
Leicestershire
LE12 8RS

Thank you – we look forward to hearing from you.

Nicky, Ian and Alison.

Contact the Go MAD® team...

If you would like to receive more information about other books in the Go MAD® range or details of other Go MAD® personal and business development products.

or...

If you are looking for new, inspiring, practical ways to develop yourself or your organisation, we offer a range of innovative Go MAD® training solutions, conference speakers, personal coaches and consultancy options.

Go MAD Ltd
Pocket Gate Farm
Off Breakback Road
Woodhouse Eaves
Leicestershire
LE12 8RS

01509 891313

www.gomadonline.com

info@gomadonline.com

Other Go MAD® books include:

Go MAD – The Art of Making A Difference
(by Andy Gilbert)
The best selling Go MAD® personal development book that explains the 7 Go MAD® key principles in detail. It contains plenty of exercises and inspirational quotations to help you focus on making a difference and increasing your success.

Go MAD About Coaching

(by Andy Gilbert & Ian Chakravorty)

This pragmatic book demonstrates step by step how the Go MAD$^®$ process can easily be used as a framework to successfully coach yourself and others. It contains over 200 powerful coaching questions, 120 tips, tools and techniques and templates of how to structure a coaching session. It also includes a free audio C.D. containing 60 minutes of coaching examples and exercises.

Go To Work On Your Career

(by Andy Gilbert, Kathryn Roberts & Nicky Frisby)

A practical career management guide based on Go MAD$^®$ research. It contains case-studies, exercises, tips, techniques and plenty of high quality questions designed to help you think about your career and make a difference.

Yes! I Can Make A Difference

(by Andy Gilbert)

A book with a difference - it hasn't been fully written yet! It contains 234 inspirational quotes and high quality questions – and lots of space for you to write in. An ideal notebook, personal diary or success journal – you choose.

Go MAD$^®$ About Meetings – 87 Ways to Make A Difference

(by Andy Gilbert & Alison Lawrence)

A handy tips booklet that provides practical ideas about applying the Go MAD$^®$ process to preparing and running meetings. Guaranteed to save time and provide focus.

59 Minutes to a Calmer Life
(by Paul McGee)
Practical strategies for reducing stress in your personal and professional life. This easy to read book is packed full of common sense, good humour, helpful advice and useful insights to help you make a difference in your life.

Go MAD® Audio products include:

The Complete Guide to Making A Difference
(by Andy Gilbert)
A six tape box set which covers everything you need to know about Go MAD® and its uses as a development process, a diagnostic tool and an analytical framework. Understand and increase your ability to apply the 7 Go MAD® key principles to develop yourself, others and your organisation. Features extracts from the original research interviews.

Go MAD® about Coaching
(by Andy Gilbert)
A six tape box set which demonstrates the powerful Go MAD® Coaching process and will increase your ability to successfully coach others. Understand the Go MAD® Framework in greater depth and how to structure a coaching session using high quality questions. Plenty of examples, tips and techniques are demonstrated and explained.

The Go MAD® Monthly Audio Magazine
A monthly source of inspiration and practical ideas to help you Go MAD®. Features the latest Go MAD® research interviews with successful people from a variety of backgrounds; development exercises; and insights from Andy Gilbert about how to apply the Go MAD® process to your life and work. This provides ideal support and further development following Go MAD® training.

Go MAD® Corporate Development Programmes include:

Go MAD® Accredited Programmes
A series of six consecutive training programmes each of which builds upon previous Go MAD® knowledge and experience to develop a high level of conscious competence in applying the Go MAD® process.

Part 1 – Yes! I Can Make A Difference   (2 days)
Part 2 – Go MAD® about Coaching   (2 days)
Part 3 – Go MAD® about Meetings and Projects (1 day)

(Parts 1, 2 and 3 are often combined to form a bespoke 4 day Accredited Coach Programme.)

Part 4 – Go MAD® Leadership Programme   (4 days over
                                                                          6 months)
Part 5 – Go MAD® Mindset Programme   ($2^{1/2}$ days)
Part 6 – Go MAD® Master Coach/Trainer   (5 days)
          Programme

Go MAD® Trainer Training for in-house licensed programmes
Parts 1,2 and 3 of the Accredited Programmes can be run internally with a license to reproduce copyright materials and use Go MAD® training videos featuring key learning points by Andy Gilbert.

Bespoke workshops and courses
These are designed to apply the Go MAD® process to specific issues that teams or organisations want to make a difference about. Recent examples include: culture change; customer care; sales; stress; career management; leadership.

Go MAD® e-learning

Over 18 hours of interactive online learning about Go MAD. The ultimate support tool with the functionality to electronically network and involve others within your organisation in the differences people want to make. It contains an artificial intelligence coaching programme to coach individuals using Go MAD® process, together with a management information system to measure the success of your training e-development activities.

Go MAD® ongoing research and development includes:

- Success profiling and a range of Go MAD® assessment tools
- Digital interactive television and e-learning
- Masterclass tele-conferencing

For current information or to be kept up to date on any of the above mentioned Go MAD® products, services or development areas please contact us and we will endeavour to help you make a difference.

If you would like to involve others in making a difference, visit the website:

www.principlefive.com

On this site you will be able to network with other people interested in making a difference. Register free to obtain a weekly Go MAD® inspirational quotation.

Notes

Notes

Notes

Notes

Notes

Notes

Notes

Notes

Notes